*The* INSPIRING TRUE STORY
*of a* WOMAN'S STRUGGLE *from* WITHIN

# An Impossible Life

RACHAEL SIDDOWAY *and* SONJA WASDEN

Copyright © 2019 Rachael Siddoway and Sonja Wasden.

All rights reserved. No part of this publication may be reproduced, distributed or transmitted in any form or by any means, including photocopying, recording, or other electronic or mechanical methods, without the prior written permission of the author.

Published by The Gap Press, LLC

An Impossible Life/ Rachael Siddoway and Sonja Wasden. —1st ed.

Cover design by: JuLee Brand for Kevin Anderson & Associates
Cover photo by Rachael Siddoway

Paperback ISBN 978-17336-194-9-3

eBook ISBN 978-1-7336194-8-6

# Contents

# CHAPTER 1

# Emergency Room, 2007

*Baton Rouge, Louisiana*

A nurse escorted me and my husband, Mitch, to the nearest room. "Wait here," she said, and the door clicked behind her. A curtain divided the room for two patients. The paper on the exam table crinkled under me, occasionally breaking the silence. I did not want to be here. I just needed to prove to Mitch that he was overreacting. I was confident that once I told the doctors everything I had gone through, they would see I simply was overstressed. That's it—nothing that the average person doesn't go through. I just wanted to get this over with and go home.

A doctor pulled the curtain back, exposing a man who was not only drunk but drugged. He could barely put a sentence together, and I could smell the alcohol. An old man and a woman, both neatly dressed, sat by the bedside, their heads down. *They must be the parents,* I thought. The doctor pulled the curtain shut, separating us once again, but the pain and disappointment were so tangible that a hospital curtain could not shut it out.

A nurse poked her head in the door. "Wow! You're stunning." She continued to stare; they always did. My sleek, blue-black hair, green eyes, and exotic features always made people do a double take, even when I was a child. Plus, I've always had a knack for putting an outfit together. Give me forty dollars at T.J. Maxx, and I can look ready to attend the Oscars. I waited for the question I had been asked a thousand times. "Where are you from?" she continued.

"Utah, but what you want to know is my nationality. It's German," I said, beating her to the punch. "Shocking, I know."

"I would have guessed Persian."

"Maybe an affair somewhere in my heritage." I forced a smile—I wanted this conversation to end. I was mismatched. My outside did not match my inside. It even disturbed me at times.

"They're ready to see you," she said, getting back on track.

I let out a slow deep breath before I followed the nurse out. She led us through light gray hallways until we entered a room with four chairs and a small coffee table. An assertive brunette with narrow eyes walked into the room. I put on my best smile and shook her hand. Perfect, a woman. She would understand my situation much better than a man.

"Hi, Mrs. Wasden. I'm a crisis worker. I'm here to evaluate you."

I leaned back into the stiff chair as I tried to escape her isolated stare.

"But I'm not in crisis."

"Then what brings you to the emergency room?"

"Just stress." I began ticking off each stressful event with my fingers. "I've moved, been living in a house that's being renovated, recently lost a hundred pounds, and I'm homeschooling my three children."

"Wow, that is a lot."

I straightened up. I knew she would understand.

"Have you ever thought about suicide?" she asked a little too casually.

I knew life was painful and the only peaceful exit led to a gravestone. Living made death look desirable. It was a solemn song everyone knew but few sang, not out loud anyway. I knew I would answer honestly—it was about time someone did.

"Who hasn't?" I raised an eyebrow.

"How often?" Her tone was similar to that of a flight attendant taking a drink order. Clearly this was routine for her.

"I don't know—just as much as the normal person does."

"Can you give me an estimate?"

"Seriously, I have no idea. Probably just as often as you." I was a bit confused by all these seemingly rhetorical questions.

"In what ways have you thought about suicide?"

She was writing everything down, which made me feel uneasy, but I needed to get through all these questions quickly so I could go home.

"Jumping off a building, driving my car into an oncoming semi-truck, standing in front of a semitruck and have it run me over"—that was my favorite one—"taking pills, drowning myself, or stabbing myself and bleeding to death." I paused. "But no guns. That's where I draw the line."

"Have you ever attempted suicide?" she asked.

I shook my head no.

"And why haven't you tried any of those things?"

"I don't think I could face God if I did," I answered openly.

She steadily looked in my eyes. "Do you want to die?"

I held her gaze as my soul echoed her question. "Yes."

She and Mitch glanced at each other. She looked back at me and stood up. I couldn't get a read on her. Was she on my side?

"Can I go home now?" I asked.

"I need to talk to the doctor. I'll be back."

She never came back. Mitch and I waited for what seemed like forever. We weren't talking, and I was getting anxious. The room was dead silent except for the soft hum of the air conditioner.

The door opened, a man and two security guards entered the room. Alarmed, I immediately stood up.

"We have a Physician Evaluation Certificate with your name on it, Mrs. Wasden. We are admitting you to the psychiatric hospital," the man stated calmly but firmly.

The room felt like it was beginning to spin. I wanted to run, but my feet were glued to the floor. Surely this was a nightmare from which I would wake at any moment and find myself safe in my bed at home. I wanted to scream but all I could get out was a raspy, "I refuse to go." I needed protection, so I turned and grabbed Mitch's arm.

"Let's go home." He said nothing. "Mitch, take me home," I pleaded. He looked at me empathetically but remained silent.

"Mrs. Wasden, we're going to help you get well."

"But I'm not sick. I'm stressed! Why won't anyone believe me?" I was getting hysterical.

"There is a van outside waiting to take you," the man stated. The two security guards were staring at me intently.

I turned to the man. "You can't force me. I won't go!"

"You're under the care of a physician, and he makes all the decisions for you. So, yes, we can force you. And we will." He held the door for me to walk out.

"You're making a big mistake. I'm not sick!" I felt like the only way out was to force an escape, which was ridiculous, considering my husband was in the room.

"Mrs. Wasden, you're actually very sick," the man responded.

"I am not crazy!" I screamed. I was tired of him saying I was "very sick" when I knew what he was suggesting.

He stood right in front of me and folded his arms. "No one is saying you're crazy, Mrs. Wasden."

"Yet you're forcing me into the psych ward." I reached out and grabbed Mitch's arm again and started shaking him. Why wasn't he saying anything, doing anything?

Mitch finally wrapped his arms around me and whispered in my ear, "You can do this. Things will be better, I promise. The sooner you go, the sooner you'll get to come home to the kids and me."

I didn't want to leave his embrace. I snuggled closer, wanting to disappear into him. But when I opened my eyes, the hospital floors were still beneath me. I leaned into Mitch. "Please don't make me do this. I can get better without going to the hospital, I promise. I'll do yoga, or deep breathing, please!" I shamelessly begged.

He stepped back and lifted my chin with his thumb, but I kept my eyes down. "Look at me, Sonja," he gently requested.

I looked up into his blue eyes and what I saw smacked me in the face. Exhaustion hung heavy in his eyes. I had been so consumed by my pain that I hadn't noticed Mitch silently suffering right beside me. The realization hit me: this hospital visit was Mitch running out of ways to make things better. Tears fell from my cheeks as I looked up at his scared but hopeful gaze. I gently put my hand on his cheek and kissed it as I whispered in his ear, "For you, Mitch, and only you." I took him in one last time—his fair skin, blond hair, and tall, lean figure—before turning around.

I straightened my cream silk blouse, twisted my diamond bracelets in place, held my head high, and went through the door. I walked down the long hallway like it was my runway, in my black designer skirt and exquisite black suede heels with a security guard on each side of me. I would not be dragged out of here. They were not going to get the best of me. If I had to leave, I'd make it look like my decision.

Nurses and patients hovered around the scene and pretended not to stare, but they did. I didn't look back, not once. I kept walking that runway and stepped into the back of a van, looking straight ahead at the bars separating me from the two men up front. The iron bars made me feel like a criminal, convicted of something that I didn't do. How did I get here?

# CHAPTER 2

# Ten Hours Earlier

Kids, come downstairs! Omi and Opa's rental car just pulled up!" I had been waiting by the window in the kitchen most of the afternoon for my parents. Their favorite treats sat on the counter—caramel popcorn and powdered sugar donuts for my dad, and Ritter Sport chocolate for my mom.

"Be careful not to bend the corner," Rachael whispered to Alex.

All three of my kids carried down the giant WELCOME sign they had made from twelve sheets of printer paper held together with Scotch tape and decorated with Magic Markers. Rachael was twelve and, being the oldest, was the natural leader and protector of her two younger brothers. Alex was ten and my most serious child but was also our peacemaker. Lincoln was seven and although the youngest, he was our most social. It didn't matter your age, he could have a conversation with anyone.

"That turned out great!" Mitch said as he helped the kids straighten the sign on the counter.

"They're here!" I yelled.

The back door opened, and there stood my mom, her small frame decorated in red. My mom's favorite color was red, a fact that would be no secret if you saw her clothes, or house, or car, or nails, or phone case. At sixty-five, she had a few white strands of hair that practically glowed against her layered brown bob.

"Sonja, is this for us?" my mom asked in her thick German accent, looking at the counter of treats.

"Yep. Hi, Dad!" I could barely finish greeting him before he picked me up in one of his famous bear hugs.

My dad was a force of nature. His life began on a small farm where he lived in a one-bedroom house with no plumbing, heating, or running water. He came from a broken home where abuse, poverty, and alcoholism were the norm. Despite all this, he managed to have a successful marriage, raise seven children, and made over twenty million dollars working in mergers and acquisitions. I grew up in Mapleton, Utah, in a 15,000-square-foot home that my dad designed himself, complete with an indoor pool and racquetball court. He lived large and spent large. From buying expensive art collections to elaborate hunting trips to Mongolia, to his beloved front row seats to the Utah Jazz, there always seemed a place for his money to go.

My dad constantly teetered on the edge of insolvency and would spend money before he had it. It was as though the tension of being broke gave him meaning and drive to do the next deal. The thrill of the next battle to be waged defined his existence. When he would wake up, the whole family could hear his King Kong routine as he pounded his chest and gave a gorilla-like call, letting the world know he was coming. Living on the edge was the only place he felt at home.

"Now, where are the three people I flew all this way to see?" My dad tucked his hands behind his suspenders and pulled them back from his big belly.

"Opa!" Rachael, Alex, and Lincoln ran out from the kitchen and jumped in his arms.

Lincoln stuck his hand in my dad's pocket. "Do you have any happiness gum in there?" My dad was known for his happiness gum; it was his trademark at church among the children and anywhere in public with strangers. Lincoln gripped two packs of Juicy Fruit gum and pulled them out with a smile.

"I don't believe this! You're robbing me blind!" My dad had a permanent laugh stuck in his voice when he talked to his grandchildren.

He scooped four more packs of gum out of his pockets. "Do you want red hot, mint, or Juicy Fruit?" He fanned all three options out like cash to Alex and Rachael.

"Red hot," Rachael called out, and my dad tossed a pack to her.

"Mint," Alex answered.

"Go long!" My dad faked a pass and then gently tossed Alex a mint pack. He had all the kids lean in for a secret. "What do you say we have Kids' Day this week?"

"Yes! Yes! Yes!" They all cheered.

Kids' Day was a holiday my dad created. It was a day where the kids got to make all the rules. They could wear pajamas all day and eat nothing but sugar. They spent most the day if not all of it at the Dollar Tree and Walmart shopping till their little hands were too full to carrying anything else. Against his better judgment, he let them drive his car for a few seconds around the neighborhood. And my dad always did some random act of kindness on those outings like buying groceries for the person in front of him. My dad was the personification of love. However, in a few short hours, he would become my number-one enemy.

"Okay, Kids' Day it is, but it's gotta be our little secret." My dad winked with his mouth wide open, but his chewed toothpick managed to stay balanced at the corner of his smile.

"So, what's the plan?" my mom asked me.

"The boys have a tennis tournament, so we'll go to that and then I have a church meeting later this evening. But the rest of the day there's no plan," I said as I filled up the boys' big water jugs. "Boys, give Opa some air and come load these in the car." I handed Alex and Lincoln their bright orange tennis bags.

"Is the gang ready to hit the road?" Mitch clapped his hands together.

"Can I pick where we go to lunch?" Rachael asked, looking up from her sketchbook.

"Sure, where should we go?" Mitch asked.

My dad leaned over. "IHOP," he whispered in Rachael's ear.

"Well, IHOP has great chocolate pancakes," Rachael said, gathering up her art books.

"Sounds like a plan, we'll stop there on the way," Mitch agreed.

"You owe me," Rachael mouthed to my dad. He tossed her another pack of gum.

Mitch, the kids, and I drove to IHOP in our car, while my mom and dad followed in their rental car. Once there, we slid into IHOP's blue vinyl benches and looked over sticky, syrup-spilled menus.

"Hi, I'm Sarah," our waitress introduced herself. "Can I get your drink orders?"

"Sarah? Sarah! That is exactly who we asked for! We heard you were the best waitress in town, so we asked specifically for you!" my dad practically yelled through the restaurant. He had done that ever since I could remember, and even now, as an adult, I still felt embarrassed. "I'll have a Coke, but take some happiness gum." He handed her a piece of Juicy Fruit, and my kids laughed.

We ate our share of pancakes and omelets and still made it to the tournament in time for the first match. Alex and Lincoln went to their assigned courts, and we found shaded benches to sit and watch.

"We're going to head back to your house. I'm tired," my mom said halfway through the boys' last match.

"Okay. We'll meet you back at the house when they're done," I said.

"Sonja, you should come with us," my dad said.

"No, I want to stay and watch the match." I kept my eyes on the ball flying across the net.

"Sonja, you need to come with us," my dad said firmly as he stood up.

I glanced at him, a bit surprised, and then turned my head back to the court. "I don't want to come."

"Sonja, come with us," he practically begged.

"You don't see your parents often. Go with them," Mitch encouraged.

"All right, all right. I'll go." I put my hands up in defeat. "I'll see you at home. Text me how the game ends." I kissed Mitch goodbye and followed my parents to their rental car, got in the back seat, and shut the door.

"You're sick, Sonja," my dad abruptly said.

"Sorry, what?" My eyebrows creased tight in confusion.

"You're sick," he repeated.

I tapped my mom's shoulder. "Is this why you came? Because you think I'm sick?" She looked into her lap and said nothing. "Well, thanks for the visit!" I tried to laugh.

"Sonja, you have been sick for a long time. It's time to get you help," my dad continued.

"No." My voice suddenly got stern. I leaned forward and jabbed my dad's arm with my pointer finger as if pushing my words into him. "I'm not sick, and I don't need help!"

Neither of them reacted, and he kept driving. I felt trapped in the back seat, like a child being forced to go to the dentist's office. "If this is why you came, you've wasted your time!" I was close to screaming.

"Mitch called us. He's going to hospitalize you," my dad stated as if he was reporting the weather forecast. My stomach dropped. Mitch never mentioned hospitalization to me. Why hadn't he talked to me about this? What other secrets was he keeping?

"Did he ask you to come?" I wanted to know. I wouldn't look at my parents; I stared out the window watching the road signs and trees pass. Numbing shock started to tingle up my legs until it covered my entire body. I was positive they were driving me straight to the mental institution, and boy, were they in for a show if they were.

"No. We came because we love you," my dad said softly.

"Well, I'm not going." They needed to know I had a choice in the matter.

My dad changed the subject and filled the car with idle conversation that I chose to ignore. I rolled my window up and down just to break up his sentences before letting their fragments fly out the window.

The car pulled up to the house, and I relaxed. Well, at least my dad wasn't entirely out of his mind. Maybe it was because he remembered I had a church meeting later that day. I happily hopped out of the car, thinking I was safe.

"Go pack. Mitch will be here soon, and then we're leaving for the hospital." My dad's voice tore through my reality. "I don't know why you look so shocked. Clearly, this is what I've been preparing you for the whole way home."

"I thought I changed your mind." I took in a big gulp of air. "I thought you were bringing me home to stay."

"To pack," he clarified.

I gritted my teeth and said, "I'm not going." I got quieter, hoping it would make them take me seriously. "I'm almost forty. You can't force me." My nose flared as my voice steadied.

"Wrong. I can get the police to take you. I can call 911 and have an ambulance take you. I can go in front of a judge and get the right to admit you, and they'll take you," he retorted. "Or you can go pack and willingly get in the car, and we can take you. You pick."

"I choose none of the above."

He sighed and pulled out a folder like he was using his last move. "These documents have all the information to get you hospitalized. It will happen." My father was the type of man that when his mind was made up, he would always go one step further than his opponent.

Mitch and the kids pulled up in the carport. I went outside to greet them as my dad followed. I shot a glance at Mitch and hated him for being behind all this. My dad could tell a bomb was about to drop and guided the kids inside. Mitch and I followed more slowly.

"You've gathered notes on me? Is this some sort of blackmail?" I angrily whispered.

Mitch tried to calm me. "Sonja, let's sit down and talk about this."

The boys set their trophies on the kitchen counter. I stepped back and looked at my dad and then Mitch. "Are you all crazy?"

"You're going to the hospital." My dad repeated the sentence like it was his own personal mantra.

"No, I'm not!" I picked up a kitchen chair and threw it against the wood floor. "I'm not going! I'm not!" I screamed so loud my own ears hurt. Mitch took the kids upstairs, hoping to protect them from the verbal debris. One by one I threw all the chairs to the ground, each one hitting the floor with a bang. I was losing control and throwing the chairs made me feel powerful. These tantrums had become more and more common over the years. My dad didn't flinch. If he wanted a knock-down, drag-out fight, I was up for it. *Fight. Fight. Fight, Sonja,* I kept telling myself. I wanted to stay in control. It was my pain and I was greedy. I didn't think I let it touch my family, especially not my children—a belief that was another illusion, as my disease had a life of its own. It reached out and affected every person so dear, so close to me. I left the room to hunt down my husband, who was upstairs, as my dad followed behind me.

I boldly walked up to Mitch. "If you hospitalize me, I will divorce you. It will be over!" My voice rang through the house.

It was nothing that he hadn't heard thousands of times before. Divorce was always my threat. Why did he continue to stay? Did he know, deep down, how much I loved, needed, and wanted him? He looked me straight in the eyes, and for the first time in our marriage he said, "That's a chance I'm willing to take."

My heart sank deep into my chest. I felt like I was going to vomit. Tears steadily rolled down my face. I was stuck. I couldn't move. *Wait,* I thought. *Wait, I love you!* But the words wouldn't come out. This massive darkness, this burden—we had always carried it together. At times, it felt heavier than Mitch and I could manage, but we always were a team.

I turned to my dad. "You did this. You're the reason my family's falling apart."

"Would you just go to the emergency room and talk with a doctor?" my dad asked. "Tell them everything, and if they say you can come home, then that will be good enough for us."

Out of the corner of my eye I saw my three children staring at me from behind my mom. They had heard everything. My children; they were my world. I had given every ounce of myself to them. I gave even when I had nothing to offer. Yet, there I stood taking more of their innocence away with every word I yelled.

I paused. My dad's plan could work. The doctor would see I was perfectly normal, and then I could come home to my family.

"You promise if the doctor says I can go home, all this talk about the hospital will stop?"

"I promise." My dad gathered me in his arms for one of his bear hugs.

"And why don't you pack a bag, just in case?" my mom added.

I put a pair of tennis shoes and one pair of sweats in a bag just to humor them. I even changed into my church clothes, proving my confidence that I would be in and out of the ER that same day, ready to attend the church meeting I had later that evening.

# CHAPTER 3

# Psych Ward

The van stopped, and my mind was instantly interrupted.

"Time to get out," one of the security guards called back to me, sliding the van door open.

My heels clicked on the cement as all three of us walked into a standard brick building. The guard on my right swiped his card, and the doors swung open like shark jaws ready to eat me alive. I craned my neck to look at the sunlight slipping through the doors behind me as they locked shut. The hallway was dark, and it felt like entering a jail. Near misses with prison were no stranger to my family, considering my grandfather almost killed a man, my dad had been indicted five times for securities fraud, and my cousin faked his own death after an elaborate counterfeiting spree. In my family we have enough material to star in our own version of *Catch Me If You Can*, although the problem is subtlety *isn't* our friend, and we *never* get away. The guards took me inside a room with a man sitting behind a desk. The man motioned for me to give him my bag. He didn't even use words. I reluctantly handed it to him and waited while he searched through it. He kept it behind the counter.

"Give me your necklace," he demanded with his hand held out.

"Why?" I couldn't help but laugh.

"It has a string in it. You could harm yourself," he said as if I was dense.

"Ridiculous," I said under my breath as I took off my pearl necklace and handed it to him.

I watched as he packed and locked my things away. The guards took me to a white concrete room with two beds and one bathroom. Nothing else was in the room except my scared self and a folded stack of clean sheets and towels balanced against my chest. I felt so alone, and the sterile empty room just added to it. I wondered what Mitch was doing right then and if he was even worried about me. Had he known how horrible this place was before he sent me here?

"Sonja Wasden?" a tall, thin woman in a lab coat read from her clipboard.

"Yes?" I quickly looked up.

"We're ready to start your examination." She took me to a doctor's office where a hospital gown lay across a bench. "Take everything off, including underwear, and put on the robe. I'll come back when you've changed."

"Why do I need to be examined?" My voice was quieter than I anticipated.

"I need to chart any bruises or cuts you have and make sure you're not hiding any drugs or weapons."

"There aren't any weapons or drugs on me. I don't need to take my clothes off to prove that."

She stopped in the doorway and sighed. "We can do this the hard way or the easy way. Your choice. I'll knock before coming in."

I looked at the light blue patterned robe draped over the bench. "Let's get this over with," I whispered to myself as I quickly slipped my clothes off and tied the robe on. The nurse came in and inspected every inch of my body. I felt violated and humiliated. I wondered what she would have done if I refused, but I felt too exhausted to put up a fight.

Another nurse came in that night. She was the first person who smiled at me. She took my vitals and sat down next to me. "Tell me what's happened," she said.

"I don't belong here." I wiped my nose against my sleeve. The tears wouldn't stop.

"It will be okay. Take these." She showed me two pills. "One is Geodon. It's a new drug. It makes you sleepy, but your body will adjust. The other pill's Lamictal. It's been around for a while." She dropped the two pills in my palm and then filled a small paper cup with water. "Here."

I swallowed the pills and hoped she knew what she was medicating me with, but regardless, it was too late. I had decided to trust her. I crawled into my hospital bed wondering what kind of people were patients here, and how many might be here by mistake, like me.

# CHAPTER 4

# Awakenings

*Brigham Young University, 1992*

U gh, Ben canceled our date for tonight," Sophie announced as she entered our college dorm room. She tossed a pair of Rollerblades on the floor.

"Please, he's probably out buying an engagement ring." I rolled my eyes and straightened my navy-and-white polka-dot scarf on top of my head before tying it in my long, loose hair. Sophie stomped her little white sneakers across the carpet and collapsed on my bed.

"I wish." Her voice was muffled by my pillow.

"So, I guess you can come with us to the movies after all." My roommate Andy excitedly hopped on my bed next to Sophie.

"Yeah, yeah, I'm coming." Sophie pretended not to be amused.

I slipped on my shoes and tossed my car keys to Andy. "You wanna drive?"

"If the other option is you driving, then, yeah. I don't want tonight being my last." Andy tucked the keys in her pocket while Sophie laughed.

"Don't encourage her." I playfully shoved Sophie.

"Sonja, you are a bad driver." Sophie laughed.

Andy pulled into the movie-theater parking lot and snagged the last good parking spot.

"I'm going to get popcorn. Save my seat." Sophie tossed her hair out of the collar of her coat. Giving her a thumbs-up, I walked into the theater with Andy.

"What's this movie about?" I asked, sitting as comfortably as I could in the old theater seats.

"*Awakenings* is a story about people who are catatonic. Then this doctor helps brings them back to life or something." Andy put her feet up on the chair in front of her.

"What do you mean catatonic?"

"They have some type of Parkinson's that makes it so they can't move or talk." Andy dropped her feet down and let Sophie walk through.

The curtains opened, and the lights dimmed. Robin Williams was cast perfectly as the doctor who saved people once unresponsive. The patients sang, danced, and talked to their families, and I found myself celebrating that there was a cure. However, the medicine was only temporary, and shortly after they all went back to being catatonic. My soul was shaken as the doctors came to the realization the patients could not be helped. If the patients never actually had a chance to be saved, which was better: to remain hopeless, or to be given hope and then lose it again, just to be reminded of what you'd lost? Even though I was not a patient, the blow of the only temporary medical treatment felt like a loss for me too. I could not imagine what it would feel like to be trapped by a lifelong illness.

"Want some?" Sophie leaned her popcorn bucket my way.

"No, thanks." I waved my hands and then threw them over my face. The lights dimly turned on and the credits projected on the screen.

"Sonja, what's wrong?" Sophie quickly put the popcorn down.

"I could never be caged by an illness like that," I said, with a few tears running down my cheeks. Sophie and Andy looked at each other.

"It was just a movie." Andy put her hand on my back, confused.

"But it was based on a true story!" I snapped.

"She's fine." Sophie smiled at the concerned couple exiting behind us.

"Let's walk to the car and get you home," Andy suggested. She and Sophie stood on each side of me as I cried my way to the passenger seat. My friends tried soothing me, but I hyperventilated through all their logic.

At the dorm, Andy asked, "What's wrong with you?"

I wish I could have told my friends what was coursing through me, but the terrified and panicked feelings had no reason to be there, and I could not piece it together, especially not while hyperventilating. I had never had a way to explain my sudden waves of emotion that would smack and knock me down, sometimes for days.

Sophie nudged her. "She's just a sensitive soul." She sat on the bed next to me and stroked my hair.

"No, this is definitely not normal," Andy told Sophie adamantly. I lay on the bed, slowly tapering down to a whimper as my loyal friends sat beside me. Our phone started ringing. Sophie popped up to answer it.

She held the phone to her chest. "Sonja, it's for you."

I lifted my face from my wet pillow and cleared my throat. "This is Sonja," I tried in my best post-cry voice.

"It's Mitch." His voice barely came through with all the noise in the background.

"Where are you?" I covered one end of the phone. "It's Mitch," I whispered to Sophie and Andy.

"What? The guy you met like six months ago?" Sophie blurted out. I put my finger to my mouth. "Sorry," she whispered.

"I'm at a gas station," Mitch answered over the commotion. Now it made sense; his car had probably broken down.

"Oh, do you need a ride?" I asked, hiding my disappointment impressively well.

"No, no. I've been trying to call you for three days. I just pulled over at a gas station pay phone and thought I'd try one last time."

"Our phone has been broken, but it just got fixed." I twisted the phone cord around my wrist.

"I was wondering if you might want to go out with me next weekend? I was thinking maybe Saturday?"

"Yes! I'd love to."

"Great, I'll pick you up Saturday at six."

I hung up the phone and turned to my friends. "Mitch just asked me on a date!" My heartbeat caught up with the excitement of the situation and quickly moved past the deep sadness the movie brought on.

"So random. You hit it off the first time you meet, and you hear from him now, six months later?" Sophie added.

The first time I saw Mitch, he was standing at my parents' front door, holding a bundle of strings that led up to a dozen colorful balloons. His family had just moved to Mapleton, and his little brother was asking my younger sister, Allyson, to a high school dance. Mitch's job was to drop the invitation off and quickly go home, but circumstance would have it that I answered the door. We talked on the doorstep till our knees hurt and I invited him to come inside. I knew I had found someone that was going to mean something to me; like two lightning bolts that finally agreed on a place to strike.

That Saturday night at six o'clock, Mitch stood on my doorstep with the same big smile that took my breath away the first time we met.

"You ready?" he asked with his hands behind his back.

"Yep!" I grabbed my coat and closed the door. Mitch backed up, hiding something behind his plaid shirt.

"What are you holding?" I suspiciously peered up at his blue eyes. He excitedly revealed two balsa wood airplanes, the kind you buy in a toy store for $1.50 and assemble yourself.

"I'm holding in my hands the best date you've ever had." Mitch smiled as we started walking toward one of the open fields on campus. "Have you ever flown one of these?" he asked, handing me an airplane.

"I can't say that I have." I touched the smooth wood.

"Good, then that means I'm going to win." He cockily grinned.

I rolled my eyes. "We'll see."

Mitch's plane glided above the trees and mine was not far behind. Spending time with him felt like being with a best friend. I was surprised a first date could feel so comfortable. He placed his hand over mine as we sat on the ledge of a fountain and talked for hours. There were no topics that felt off limits.

"My dream is to be able to fit everything I own in my car, so I can go anywhere I want," he said.

"So, tell me." I leaned back on my hands and looked at him. "What career do you see for yourself in the future?"

Mitch twirled a blade of grass in his fingers and looked at me. "That's easy. I want to be a history professor."

"I think you'd be good at that." I put my head on his shoulder. I knew at the end of that night I had found my person. He walked me to the door, and I put my key in the lock.

"Thanks for the date. I had a lot of fun with you," I said.

"Yeah, I get that a lot. All the girls like me. I'm kind of a catch." He shrugged.

I couldn't help but laugh at his confidence.

"I had a great time with you, too." He kissed my cheek.

## CHAPTER 5

# Psych Ward

*Day One*

B reakfast is ready," a nurse called into my room.
I opened my eyes and saw the same white, cracked ceiling I had seen when I went to bed. Ugh, it was not a dream. The people here were part of a group to which I didn't want to belong. I wanted to stay in my room all day, but I knew it wouldn't be long before another nurse would notice I had not left. Still, I lay on my back, letting the seconds roll by slowly.

"Sonja, come out for breakfast." The nurse stood in the doorway with her hands on her hips.

"I'm not hungry," I lied.

"I'm not leaving until you come out. You have to eat with your medication." The firmness in her voice told me I wasn't the first patient to refuse her that day. I got out of bed and stopped at the doorframe. "Come on," she insisted as she walked ahead of me but looked back to make sure I was following, and unfortunately for me, I was. "Breakfast is right over there."

I grabbed a tray and stayed a few feet behind the line in front of me, scanning the options. Nothing looked terribly safe except the packaged oatmeal. I slid my tray past the bruised fruits that were clearly past their expiration date and the buffet of hard donuts and muffins not protected by sneeze glass. And judging from the patients in front of me, sneeze glass was needed.

The tables were filled with people of all ages eating their breakfast. I tried looking for an empty table but quickly realized there were none. I sat next to a young blond girl playing with a deck of cards. "Hi," I shyly greeted her. She looked up from the cards and turned toward me. The other half of her hair was pink and yellow. She barely glanced at me before turning back to her cards. I tore the paper off my oatmeal packet and scooted to the edge of my chair.

Diagonally from me sat a gray-haired man, chanting, "The man in the mirror is a handsome man. The man in the mirror is me." He pulled out a piece of paper and began vigorously writing the words he spoke, getting louder and louder. "The man in the mirror is a handsome man. The man in the mirror is me. The man in the mirror is a handsome man! The man in the mirror is me!" He caught me staring and paused.

I smiled at him. He looked down and went back to his writing and repetitious chanting. I'd be sitting at a different table tomorrow.

"Line up for meds!" the nurse yelled. People started shuffling around in the conference room like soldiers gathering shoulder to shoulder before their general. I squeezed into line and watched the people in front of me. The nurse handed each of them a small paper cup with medicine in it; they swallowed their pills and opened their mouths for the nurse to look inside. It was my turn. The nurse handed me a small paper cup with two pills in it.

"What are you giving me?" I asked.

"Geodon and Lamictal." They were the same pills from the night before. I tilted the cup back and swallowed them.

"Open," the nurse said on cue. I opened my mouth, and she moved onto the next person. These antipsychotic pills meant nothing to me at the time, but later they would mean everything to me. They would torture me and save my life all at the same time.

I went to my room and felt a type of sleepiness I had never experienced before. It slowly took control of my whole body, and it felt scary as I slowly slipped into unconsciousness. The next thing I knew

I was being escorted to the conference room. A smartly dressed man walked in and parked himself in a chair next to me. "I'm Dr. Barry. I'll be your psychiatrist while you're here."

"What time is it?"

"Three o'clock."

"I've slept all day?"

"Yes. That's one of the medicine's side effects. Your body will adjust. So, you're renovating a house." He raised his eyebrows. "That's ambitious."

"That's why I'm so stressed. Most of the flooring has been ripped out and we have to tiptoe up the stairs so we don't step on the nails sticking through the wood. We eat off cardboard boxes that haven't been opened yet and live in a constant cloud of sawdust."

"And you're homeschooling your kids?" Dr. Barry commented, looking through my file.

"Yes, because the schools are pretty rough here in Louisiana. I thought enrolling them in public magnet schools would be better, but boy, was I wrong." I slid my hands down my lap. "When we got to my sons' school the first day, I thought I had taken a wrong turn. The school was right next to boarded-up houses and people sitting on their porches smoking weed and selling drugs. Although my daughter's school was brand-new, the first day we witnessed a kid pushed against his locker getting handcuffed. The armed guards patrolling the hallways weren't exactly a comfort."

"Why aren't your kids in private school? Your husband's vice president at a large health system."

"My husband's secretary informed him that's what most people do, but by that time they were full. Right now we're on a waiting list. I've felt tremendous pressure to educate my kids, so they can compete in college. I have cried and prayed about the enormity of it all."

"I'm sure you and your husband will figure it out," he said to ease my anxiety. His eyes briefly scanned the last parts of my file. "Let's talk about why you're here." He closed the folder and looked at me. "Do you want to die?"

"I'm sure it's all in your notes. But yeah, I do, like most people. I've recently thought it might be nice to fly to an orphanage in a remote part of Africa to help take care of the kids and drink some of the water there. I might get dysentery or a mosquito bite that gives me malaria and die. God couldn't judge me for that."

"Sonja, you'll feel differently soon."

"I don't belong here."

"No one belongs here. This place is just a pit stop." He looked at me. "The only permanent residents are the doctors, so I'm the only person who *does* belong here." He smiled.

"I don't need the pit stop, is what I mean. I'm stressed, but I'm not crazy," I said sternly.

Dr. Barry paused before saying anything. He propped his chin over his palm. "You know, Sonja, I've read your file a few times, and I can't help but think that you must know you're sick."

I sat up. "Excuse me?"

"I've been doing this a long time, and most untreated people with a mental illness believe life is brutal and just hell for everyone, even though it's not. Have you ever felt that?"

"I haven't because I know life is hell for everyone. Is this a trick question?" I looked at him. "And to be clear, I'm nothing like the rest of the patients here. And you shouldn't assume I am."

Dr. Barry calmly looked at his pad and wrote a few notes. "I think we're done for today." He got up and left the conference room, and I sat terrified.

As I was walking back to my room, a young man in his thirties, wearing jeans and a button-up shirt, came out of his room carrying his packed bags. He stopped and introduced himself.

"Hi, I'm Doug. I was taking care of my sick father and got depressed. I checked myself into this place. I've only been here two days, and I'm already leaving."

"You're leaving after two days?" My eyes widened.

"The only warning I have for you is Jane. She's one of the counselors here, and she's a real bitch. Pray you don't get her." He slapped me on my back. "Don't worry. You'll be one of those who gets out real quick. Trust me, two days, tops!"

I continued down the hallway feeling more hopeful. The door to my room was propped open.

"Your roommate just arrived," a nurse said, stepping out.

"Oh," was all my nerves allowed me to reply.

I opened the door and saw a short, slender woman with dirty blond hair folding some T-shirts on the other bed.

"Hi, I'm Sonja."

She dropped the white shirt she had just finished folding and turned around. "Oh, hi! I'm Sydney!"

We didn't shake hands; we only smiled. There was a knock at the door.

"It's time for introductions in the conference room," the nurse let us know. Sydney and I walked out and into the room where a group of people was sitting in a circle on the floor.

"We're all going to introduce ourselves and say what brought us here." The nurse looked at the man next to her to start.

"M-m-my n-n-name is Brent." He paused and stuttered before getting to the next sentence. "I-I-I'm here because of schizophrenia."

A woman in her sixties fidgeted in her seat. "I struggle with suicidal feelings and drugs. I shot my son-in-law with a rifle because he cheated on my daughter. Luckily, he survived. I was high as a kite when it happened."

Next, it was Sydney's turn. I wondered what had brought her here.

"I'm Sydney, and I'm here because of attempted suicide."

Wow, she had attempted it. I had contemplated, even fantasized, about suicide millions of times, but had never tried it. Before I could fully process her answer, the room got quiet, and the nurse leading the discussion stopped her note taking and looked up at me.

"Oh, sorry, I'm Sonja, and I'm here because of stress."

The nurse wrote in her notebook, and the next person continued. Depression, schizophrenia, attempted suicide, bipolar, and electric shock treatment were just a few of the reasons mentioned. At the end, everyone stood and held hands for a prayer. It was a prayer I had never heard before but would never forget.

God grant me the serenity to accept the things I cannot change;
Courage to change the things I can;
And wisdom to know the difference.

Sydney and I went through most of that day without talking to each other. That night we brushed our teeth in the shared bathroom and got into our beds.

"What did you do before you came here?" I asked in the dark room.

"I'm an elementary-school teacher. What about you?"

"I'm a mom. I have three kids."

"I don't have kids. Is it nice?"

"Yeah." I turned over on my side and closed my eyes. My heart burned; I missed Mitch and the kids so much. I silently cried myself to sleep thinking about them. This lonely and desperate destination was all too familiar.

# CHAPTER 6

# Broke

*Ann Arbor, Michigan, 1994*

Welcome to Michigan!" Mitch cheered as we sped past the state sign. I leaned forward on my lap as another wave of nausea hit me.

"Yay." I moaned, my face between my knees. Six months pregnant and sitting on my un-air-conditioned U-Haul throne, I could not muster much excitement.

"How are we holding up?" Mitch rubbed my back.

"Not great. Let me know when we're close to our apartment." I felt sick, not only because of the pregnancy but also because we were driving closer and closer to our new home and farther and farther away from my childhood home. This would be the first time I had ever lived more than twenty minutes away from my parents. I was twenty-two and had only been married a year and a half. We had just packed up everything we owned to move to Ann Arbor, Michigan, for Mitch to get his master's in health administration. We were completely broke and planned on living off credit cards until we could get established. Part-time jobs and student loans would get us through the next two years. And on top of all that I was going to be a mom. All those facts sank deep, layering like sediment in my bones.

"All right, Sony, we're in our new neighborhood." I looked over the dashboard and saw children playing on the playground surrounded by on-campus housing, part of a cookie-cutter set all lined up right next to each other.

"This will be our home for the next two years!" Mitch exclaimed. He always had a natural optimism, especially in the face of new adventures. While I liked that trait in him, I worried about being ready for an adventure this large.

After our U-Haul was emptied of all of our belongings, Mitch and I sat in silence among the cardboard boxes in our new apartment. I was completely rattled.

"Are you hungry?" he asked, breaking the silence.

"Yeah, but we don't have any food."

"Let's go to Denny's and get something," Mitch suggested. I leaned my head on his shoulder, feeling somewhat comforted that we had a plan, even if it was just for tonight's dinner.

At Denny's, we sat at a table waiting to order. "Can you order for me?" I asked Mitch. "I'm going to call my dad real quick."

"Sure, don't take too long."

I needed to talk to my dad. He always knew what to say when I felt lost. I didn't have enough coins, so I called collect from the pay phone. I gripped the black handle waiting for someone to accept the charges as it rang.

"Hallo?" My mom's familiar German accent echoed into the phone.

"Hey Mom, is Dad home?"

"No, but did you make it to Michigan already?" If my dad wasn't home, I planned on being strong and letting my mom know we got here safe, but my heart broke as soon as I heard her voice.

"Mom!" I sobbed.

"Sonja, what's wrong?" she asked, concerned.

"I don't want to be an adult anymore. I don't want to be pregnant. I don't want to live in Michigan. I want to be a sixteen-year-old kid again. Safe, sleeping in my room with nothing to worry about except my weekend plans."

My mom cut in. "You'll be fine, Sonja."

"I'm scared. I'm scared to be a mom. We have no health insurance, no jobs, and no money," I cried.

"Sonja, life is hard for everyone. Oh no! My chicken on the stove is burning. I've got to go, but give me your phone number once your phone is hooked up. Love you, tschüss."

As usual, no time for tears. My mom couldn't comfort me, even though she knew what it felt like to leave everything behind. She and her family had escaped East Germany and fled to West Germany when she was a child. Her father was captured during World War II and died in a Russian prison camp, and her mother struggled to keep all five kids from starvation, tragically losing her newborn baby boy. My mother met my father in Germany while he was a missionary there. At the age of nineteen, knowing very little English, she left her mother and country. She came to America, where she and my dad were later married. Her situation seemed much harder than mine, but she would not let down her stoic German guard to sympathize with me. My mother was a good person, and we loved each other deeply but struggled at times to understand each other.

I hung up the phone and went back to Mitch. He saw my red eyes and wrapped me in his arms.

I leaned into his chest. "I don't think I can do this."

"Sony, of course you can do this. I married Superwoman." I teared up again. "People have babies and go to school every day. We can do this." He pressed his lips against my forehead. "We should probably start job searching so we can get health insurance." He looked at me gently, hoping the statement wouldn't upset me.

"We qualify for government help," I pointed out again, even though I knew it wouldn't change anything.

"Welfare is for people that literally have no options. We still have options." Mitch had grown up in a family that believed taking any type of government help went against their morals.

"We're broke with a baby on the way, and even with jobs we still qualify for government programs. I'm a humanities major. There aren't many jobs in my field with health benefits, and we can't afford to have this baby."

"I know it's scary. Can we at least try?"

In the following days, Mitch and I applied for several jobs. I found a job opening for a part-time phlebotomist with hours from 5 A.M. to 9 A.M. that offered full health insurance benefits. If I got this job not only would we have health insurance, but Mitch could watch our baby while I worked and we wouldn't have to pay for day care. I took the bus to the University of Michigan determined to find out who oversaw the phlebotomy department and to get the job.

However, there were two big problems. First, I had no experience as a phlebotomist, and second, I had been terrified of needles since I was a little girl. My stomach clenched at the thought of ever putting one in a human. The desperate need for health insurance drove me forward since my baby would be born in less than three months.

The hospital felt as big as a major airport; I could barely navigate myself to the elevator. I walked into a room with a large table with chairs surrounding it and a wall covered with lab trays full of needles and empty vials ready to be filled with blood. I took a big breath and turned to the only person sitting in the room. "Is the person in charge of the phlebotomy department here?" I asked.

"She just left, but she'll be back. I can't promise when, though. Should I take a message for her?"

I glanced at the tubes of blood lying on a counter waiting to be sent to the lab. I felt faint and took a deep breath. I hated the sight of blood.

"No, it's okay. I'll wait." I sat in one of the black plastic chairs, feeling entirely out of my element. I turned my back to the wall of needles and vials, deciding that staring at the bare white wall was a better option. How in the world would I get this job? I studied art. I had no medical background at all. And what if I got the job? How was I going to overcome my fear of needles and draw blood from another human being? Just the thought of it filled me with dread so strong it made me physically sick. I waited for three hours before a lady walked into the lab.

"She's here," the woman informed me. I quickly stood up.

"You must be the head of the phlebotomy department!" I shook her hand firmly.

"Yes, I am." She looked at me, a bit perplexed.

"I'm Sonja Wasden and I need to work here. I don't have any experience, but I will get any certificate or training I need to become a phlebotomist!" My enthusiasm clearly took her by surprise.

"Normally we don't hire people who haven't been trained, but on very rare occasions we've trained our staff."

I grabbed hold of my sliver of a chance at being one of those rare few. "I'll do whatever it takes. I'm one hundred percent committed."

"Have you filled out an application?"

"Yes, I have."

"I'll look over your application and get back to you in two weeks." I shook her hand and left, hoping I had made somewhat of a good impression on her, since my application wasn't going to set me apart in the least.

Mitch got a job at a warehouse loading trucks for Kmart. It was part-time with no benefits and didn't pay nearly enough. We were running low on money, and our student loans were not coming in for another six weeks. While we hadn't heard from the hospital yet, I did get a call back for a waitress position at the Olive Garden.

"What days would you be available to work?" the manager interviewing me for the position inquired.

"All the days!" I eagerly responded. "Except Sundays. I can't work Sundays because of my religion, but I promise I'll work hard."

The manager paused and rubbed his chin. "Usually new staff without seniority pick up holidays and weekends. But you seem motivated, and you'd be good with customers, so I'll take a chance on you."

"Thank you so much. You won't be sorry." I shook his hand vigorously.

On my first day, I was handed a brown apron as my uniform. I tied it over my very pregnant stomach and started waiting tables. That day four tables asked about the alcoholic drinks. Since I grew up as a member of the Church of Jesus Christ of Latter-day Saints and had never been around alcohol, I didn't know any beer or wine names. I had never even tasted alcohol. So, I stared at customers bewildered each time I took down a drink order.

My manager finally pulled me aside a few hours into my first shift. "Jeez, who doesn't know what a Heineken or a Bloody Mary is? Where have you been hiding, under a rock? Go home and memorize these!" He handed me the Olive Garden drink menu.

Despite my swollen ankles and lack of knowledge about alcohol, working at the Olive Garden was a great way to keep my mind off waiting to hear back from the hospital. Back home, I sat on our couch, quizzing myself on all the specialty beers.

"Stella Artois, Corona, Heineken."

"Sony, what are you doing?" Mitch laughed, picking up one of my flash cards.

"Trying to keep my job." I flipped over the next card. "Peroni."

"Let me help you." He took the stack of cards and started quizzing me. "All right, there are six specialty beers, and three of them are in green bottles. Which three?"

"I don't know, Stella Artois?"

"Yep, that's one." He waited for the next two while holding the flash card up to his nose.

I shrugged. I had no idea.

"Okay, let's try a memorization trick. Green is the color of aliens, and the last two beers have foreign names."

"Heineken and Peroni?"

Mitch nodded. He quizzed me on margaritas, wines, and cocktails, and by the end of the night, I felt like a pro. Because of my drink knowledge, I kept my job at the Olive Garden, which meant Mitch's and my new after-work routine would consist of us sitting on our living room floor counting out my tips.

One afternoon, while Mitch and I sat with bowls of cereal in our laps, counting quarters and dollar bills stacked an inch high in separate piles, our phone rang.

"Hello? Yes, she's here." Mitch handed me the phone. "It's the hospital!" he whispered.

I stood in shock as the department manager on the other line gave me the best news ever. "Thank you! Thank you so much! I'll be there!" I turned to Mitch and jumped in his lap, knocking over a pile of quarters. "I got the job!" I screamed. It literally felt like we had won the lottery.

He squeezed me tight. "I'm so proud of you! You're going to be fantastic."

I showed up for my first day of training in a white lab coat, and to my surprise got to practice on a fake arm. Thank goodness. Every day it got a little easier, and the needles and equipment started to get less frightening. After five weeks, my trainer informed me I would need to start practicing on a coworker. Joe volunteered. He sat in the chair, and I tied the tourniquet around his upper arm. I felt for a good vein and took a deep breath. I tore open an alcohol swab and uncapped a needle. My hands were shaking as I hovered the needle over his vein.

"Any moment now, Sonja. My arm is getting a little numb," Joe said.

"I need a minute." I set the needle down and took the tourniquet off.

"You can do this." My trainer patted my back. I picked the needle back up and felt for a vein. "Stop, you need to open a new needle since you set that one on the counter," she reminded me.

"It's okay, Sonja. Even if you miss, just go for it," Joe encouraged.

*I'm doing it for my baby,* I kept repeating in my head. I uncapped the needle for the last time and tore open another alcohol pad. I felt for a vein, wiped his arm with the alcohol, and stuck the needle in his arm.

"I did it!" I looked down at my hand holding the needle in his arm and panicked. I quickly pulled the needle out. Blood started spraying out of Joe's arm, going everywhere. He ripped off the tourniquet and grabbed a handful of gauze.

"What happened?" my trainer yelled. I looked at the bloody needle in my hand and quickly set it down. My chest collapsed.

"She left the tourniquet on." Joe laughed, wiping up his arm, the table, and the tray next to him.

"I'm so sorry." My voice shook.

"You need more practice," my trainer stated.

"Am I fired?"

"No. We'll send you to the outpatient area to learn how to draw blood on healthy people. You definitely aren't ready to work with sick people."

She was right. I needed more training. I, Sonja Wasden, was not going to go down as a quitter. I needed to be good on the toughest cancer patients whose veins had turned rock solid from chemotherapy. In time, not only did I learn to tolerate needles and become an adequate phlebotomist but also, over a few months, I became good enough to draw blood on even the sickest patients at the hospital. One man dying from cancer told me if he had a bag of gold coins, he would give them to me because, unlike other phlebotomists, I only had to poke him once. The triumph of overcoming my fear of blood and needles got tucked deep away in my heart. At that time, little did I know I would face fears of a far greater magnitude. Yet, this small victory was evidence: even when I was desperate, I could do hard things, even stay alive, for the children that would come into my life.

Several months after arriving in Michigan, I woke up in the middle of the night feeling something wet beneath me. "Mitch, I think my water broke!" We rushed to the hospital, not really understanding how the whole process was supposed to work. During the delivery, we had a scare when the cord was wrapped around our baby's neck. The doctor and nurses worked quickly to revive our bluish-red baby and, in the end, our beautiful baby girl was healthy and well.

The day you hold your baby for the first time is one no mother forgets. I remember the nurses bringing me a small pink blanket where my dark-haired daughter, Rachael, slept. It only took that tiny instant of holding my baby to know I would never let anything harm her, and I would die for her. At night I refused to let the nurses take her away. I made sure she slept next to me. My dad called me the Lioness because I was so protective of my children, but the fierce loyalty I felt for that small baby only grew stronger over the years and tripled by the time I had my two sons. The things Mitch and I had to do to provide for our family that very next year stretched our faith in ways I could not have predicted.

I stood next to Mitch, balancing one-and-a-half-year-old Rachael on my hip, six months pregnant with baby number two. Tears streamed down my face as an older gentleman looked over our only car, a red Chevy Nova.

"This car will be perfect for my high school son." The man beamed.

Mitch was about to graduate with a fellowship lined up with Lovelace Hospital in Albuquerque, New Mexico, but we had run out of money and our credit cards were maxed out. There was no money to pay rent. We had been eating croutons, chips, and cereal for weeks. Our only option was to sell our car. Mitch and I had no idea how we would get to Albuquerque from Michigan or how he would get to work since we were selling our only means of transportation. The emotional darkness that had steadily been growing inside of me the last year only took on more strength as fear for our future grew.

"So, two thousand dollars?" the man inquired.

"Yes," Mitch confirmed.

My dad lived in a multimillion-dollar home, yet was strapped for cash. He had his house mortgaged to the hilt. Nothing unusual, it was always feast or famine for him. Unfortunately for me, it was a famine time in his life, so my parents were unable to help. Mitch had too much pride to ask his parents for help because they were so intent on doing things for yourself. So, the car it had to be.

"Sold!" the man said as he counted out two thousand dollars in Mitch's hands.

Relief came two months later when Mitch's parents gave us their old blue Honda Civic that had over two hundred thousand miles on it and a trunk that was strapped down with duct tape. It was a beater for sure, but one we were thrilled to own. It was a blessing.

# CHAPTER 7

# Psych Ward

*Day Two*

A nurse brought me to the conference room for group therapy where a short, broad woman had her feet firmly planted in the center of the room.

"My name is Jane, and I'll be your counselor for the rest of your stay here."

I couldn't help but roll my eyes. Just my luck, Jane was my counselor, the very woman I was warned about.

Only five minutes into class and the recurring, drug-induced, sleepy feeling overwhelmed me. It was like a wave, the way it pulled me under against my will. I had to get to a bed right away, or I would pass out on the table in front of everyone. I stood up and ran out of the room. I collapsed on my bed. I didn't want to sleep; it was morning, and I had just woken up. I fought it, but the more I fought, the more panicked I felt. Shaking and crying, I realized this was just another battle I was losing as sleep overtook me.

I felt a person shaking me. I could barely open my eyes. "Lunch!" a nurse screamed.

My eyes flew open and then closed just as fast. I often wondered why the nurses would try to wake up a drugged person they knew couldn't get out of bed even if they wanted to. Yet day after day they would shake me and scream, "Lunch!"

Once I woke up, I lay in my bed, amazed that I could open my eyes. I took a deep breath, sat up, and I could finally control my body again. I stepped out into the conference room where everyone usually gathered. I looked around the empty room. Where did everyone go? I glanced at the clock and did a double take. It was 1 P.M. I had slept the whole day again but had woken up early enough for outside time. I was thrilled! People started walking out of their classes and headed for the doors. It was most everyone's favorite part of the day. Since all entries stayed locked, we could not go outside unless it was designated "outside time," which happened once a day for thirty minutes. I perked up and started following the group out. I needed some fresh air, the sun on my face, to look up at the sky.

"If you have your name on the board, you aren't allowed to join outside time," a nurse announced. "Allison, Jared, Brad," she listed off and they left the group and went to their rooms. I was right at the doors when the nurse shouted, "Sonja!" I turned around, convinced it wasn't me. Was there another Sonja? I waited for someone else to appear. "Sonja!" the nurse yelled louder.

"Me?" I said, stepping out of the line.

"Yes, your name is on the board." She called the last couple of names. "Alex, Brent." It couldn't be true. But sure enough, as I looked at the board, there was my name. I approached the nurse's desk.

"Why is my name on the board? I haven't broken any rules."

"You didn't attend your classes."

"Are you kidding?" I laughed.

"No. You are not allowed to go outside," the nurse insisted.

"But that's because you drugged me!" I yelled. My cheeks felt hot.

"You're not allowed to go outside. You missed class. Sorry." She wasn't sorry.

"And here I thought depressed people were supposed to get exercise." I glared at her.

"Are you saying you're depressed?"

I was ready to explode. I burst into tears. I was being treated like a child that couldn't go out for recess. The only difference was I had not done anything wrong! The tears wouldn't stop, but the nurse at the desk went on with her business while I stood there crying.

"I don't know why I'm here! I could just as easily be drugged and sleep at my own house!" I went to my room and slammed the door shut. Sydney quietly opened the door and walked in.

"Don't worry, Sonja, tomorrow you'll get outside time. I'll make sure of it." She smiled.

"Thanks. But you're going to miss your outside time. Go," I said. She hugged me before she left.

The next day she tried to keep her promise. The only problem was outside time was before lunch, and I was passed out in bed because of my meds. Sydney and Brent dragged me outside. I made it as far as the bench before passing out.

"You looked like a drunk on a park bench," Sydney told me afterward. "Have you ever been drunk?"

"Nope. Never."

"Never?"

"I don't need to drink to embarrass myself. One time I went to a karaoke diner with my husband and some of our friends. My friend dared me to go up and sing. So, I did. I went up and belted out Abba's song 'Waterloo.' I danced and sang my butt off. I was horrible. I can't sing. But that didn't stop me, or other people, from standing up and cheering for me. My husband and friends were laughing so hard they were crying. After the song was done, I walked back to our table, high-fiving people as I went, and a guy yelled to the waiter, 'I want what she's drinking!'"

"Well, there you have it, you're a sober drunk." Sydney high-fived me.

\*

Visiting hours were in twenty minutes, and I couldn't wait to see Mitch. My children were not allowed to come and visit me. I sat watching the clock for the big hand to hit 6:30 and then he would be permitted in. Then I realized that same sleepy feeling I felt in the morning was washing over me again. The drugs they had given me after dinner were kicking in. *Stay awake just fifteen more minutes,* I told myself. Then I could see Mitch. I said a prayer pleading with God to help me stay awake, but it was not working. In anger, I got up and focused all my energy on getting to the nurse's desk.

"How could you give me pills that would knock me out right before visiting hours? How could you do it?" I was barely getting the words out.

The nurse said nothing. I was sliding down to the floor with my fingers gripping the desk, trying to stand up, but my body just kept on sliding. The next thing I heard was Mitch's soft voice.

"Sonja?"

Was it really Mitch? There he was at my bedside! I wanted to throw myself into his arms and sob. I tried to tell him everything about this place and what they had done to me, but my eyelids kept falling shut. I fought to lift them over and over. It was a blur, but I saw a nurse walk in and tell Mitch that no one was allowed in the patient's room except the patients and doctors. He kissed my hand as he got up to leave.

"Wait." The word came out slow as I tried with everything I had to get out of bed.

Mitch helped me up and dragged me out of my room. I couldn't keep my body upright. I was like a rag doll sliding to the floor slipping through his fingers. I was falling asleep on him. I kept fighting to stay awake. I had to talk to him. I struggled and fought, but sleep took me over, and I didn't get to speak with Mitch. He later told me that the nurses put me back to bed. After he talked to them, they allowed me to take my medicine after visiting hours from then on. But my morning meds were nonnegotiable.

# CHAPTER 8

---

# Steak Knives

*Mandeville, Louisiana, 1999*

S teak knives were my favorite. I had them all over the house: on my nightstand by my bed, on my computer desk, by the couch in the living room, in the bathroom on the counter. My knives were an essential part of my existence. My five-year-old daughter, Rachael, would take them and hide them, waging a battle she was never going to win.

I sat at my computer desk, praying for the pain to pass, praying to have the strength to endure it, but the pain raged on. I held my knees, curled in the fetal position. My body shook as I cried out in anguish. I wanted the pain to stop more desperately during those moments than any other time in my life, even though the outcome never changed. Cutting myself was the only thing I could think to do in those moments. I just needed something to interrupt the emotional pain signals going to my brain. By cutting my feet and legs, I'd get a brief amount of relief from the emotional pain as the physical pain signals took their place.

I reached up toward the steak knife on my desk—the only medicine I had to dull the agony. I grabbed it and started to cut the bottoms of my feet. It stung. The times the pain got bad enough to cut it felt like tidal waves were swallowing me, rolling me through an angry sea. I fought for air, but it was going to suffocate me, and I was willing to do anything to make the pain stop. I cut more and deeper, wanting that sweet stinging to interrupt the tides that continued to drown me. My feet started to bleed, but I couldn't stop. I cut until I took a breath, and then cut again, until I could relax.

I grabbed a towel off the desk. Being prepared was key. I wiped the blood from my feet and put my socks on. Oh, crap, my foot. I must have cut too deep. I limped out of the computer room. I told everyone I suffered from severe cases of ingrown toenails, a lie which always covered up my random limping episodes rather nicely. I rinsed the knife off and watched my blood swirl down the drain.

Moving was one of the things that triggered my intense pain. We had just moved from Albuquerque, New Mexico, to Mandeville, Louisiana, for Mitch's job promotion. Little did I know we would continue to move as Mitch climbed his career ladder. I also had just had my third child, Lincoln. Doctors thought my depression stemmed from the baby blues, but I knew my pain ran much deeper.

# CHAPTER 9

# Psych Ward

*Day Three, Afternoon*

My day started in the afternoon with Dr. Barry after I had awoken from my drug-induced sleep.

"Tell me about your childhood."

"I grew up in a loving home with a mom, dad, and six siblings whom I adore. My mom always made home-cooked meals and kept a clean house. My dad spent hours teaching us life skills in front of his white marker board like he was a coach grilling us about the right plays to make in life. He wanted his posterity to have a poverty and alcoholic-free life. He fought for it. I spent my childhood summers in Utah tubing down the canal and lying on the grass looking at the clouds. And I loved playing night games, like kick the can, with my friends."

"That sounds pretty ideal." Dr. Barry smiled.

"It was perfect."

"Why do you cut yourself?" He started flipping through more of my file.

"Don't tell me you don't understand why people cut, Doctor. It's completely logical." I was annoyed at his question.

"Explain how hurting yourself on purpose is logical."

"Because you're in so much emotional pain that physical pain interrupts emotional pain. I'm trying to get out of the pain that is worse, not inflict more."

"So, would you be okay if your children self-harmed?"

"Absolutely not!"

"Then why is it okay for you to do it? Why aren't you using different methods to handle your pain?"

"I haven't found any. But I've searched. Trust me, I've been searching. I never said I thought it was right to self-harm. I only explained why I think people do it."

"Do you think there might be something, even in the smallest degree, wrong with you?" Dr. Barry looked at me earnestly.

I had felt like there was something off for the last twenty-three years, but I could never figure out what it was. The fact that my husband and dad had brought me to the psych ward shocked me. Just because I didn't feel normal did not mean I had to be sent here. I knew I was a little off, but I also knew I was not insane.

"Maybe," was all I would timidly offer Dr. Barry. I knew in a place like this, the smallest admission could lead to a lifetime diagnosis, and I was not going to set myself up.

"It's the sickness, Sonja. People who are sick self-harm." Obviously, Dr. Barry felt the need to spell it out for me.

"I'm not sick!" I panicked like a child refusing to fill an aching cavity.

Dr. Barry sighed and looked at his feet. "Do you think you feel threatened by the idea of being mentally ill . . . because you know it's true?"

Rage filled me. "I don't know what I have, but I know, whatever it is, it's not going to be cured by being here!"

"Do you sleep well?" Dr. Barry continued ignoring my outburst.

I breathed in and out, trying to relax. "That's all I ever do since I've been here."

"What about before you came?"

"I would sleep maybe a couple of hours at night. I would constantly wake up, and sleeping pills were no help. My mind has a hard time shutting down," I said rather aggressively.

"The Geodon will help with that," he informed me.

"When do I get to go home?" I held back tears.

"Soon enough." He put his hand on my shoulder and left.

I sat in class and squeezed my lips as tightly as I could, afraid they would betray me and reveal my every thought. I didn't want to lose my outside time. Yet, my entire being wanted to stand up and scream, "Why are you giving me a list of famous people who have a mental illness? Please give me a list of ordinary people who have a mental illness and found a way to live with it!"

It seemed the mentally ill that I knew were in two camps: the mentally ill who could not hold down jobs and were homeless, and those who were rich and famous. Even though I didn't think I was mentally ill, I still wanted the counselors to show me how I could live a normal life in the middle of these two extremes. I just wanted to be a mom who could shower, plan birthday parties without pain, do laundry, and take peaceful walks on Sundays with my family. What was the secret to doing that?

I continued to remain silent. I kept all these thoughts to myself, realizing that no one in this room, not even the doctors and nurses, had the answer. Besides, I wouldn't let famous people, or anyone, make me lose my outside time. Oh, how I longed to be outside and feel the sun on my face. I gripped the paper harder and forcefully stared at it as we went over the massive list of people.

Abraham Lincoln—severe clinical depression

Angelina Jolie—depression; self-harm

Ben Stiller—bipolar disorder

Billy Joel—alcoholism; depression

Britney Spears—bipolar disorder; postnatal depression

Carrie Fisher—bipolar disorder; substance abuse

Drew Barrymore—clinical depression; alcoholism; substance abuse

Edgar Allan Poe—clinical depression (speculated); alcoholism

Elton John—substance abuse; bulimia nervosa

Ernest Hemingway—clinical depression

Georgia O'Keeffe—clinical depression

Harrison Ford—clinical depression

Heath Ledger—depression; anxiety; sleep deprivation

J.P. Morgan—bipolar disorder

James Taylor—clinical depression; bipolar disorder

John Quincy Adams—clinical depression

Judy Garland—clinical depression; substance abuse

Leo Tolstoy—clinical depression; hypochondriasis;
    alcoholism; substance abuse

Ludwig van Beethoven—bipolar disorder

Marilyn Monroe—clinical depression

Mel Gibson—bipolar disorder

Ozzy Osbourne—bipolar disorder

Pablo Picasso—clinical depression

Princess Diana—bulimia nervosa; depression

Robin Williams—clinical depression

Sheryl Crow—clinical depression

Sting (Gordon Sumner)—clinical depression

Vincent van Gogh—clinical depression; bipolar disorder
    (speculated)

Winston Churchill—bipolar disorder

I held the papers over my face and wanted to scream. We filed out of the classroom, and I threw the documents in the trash on my way out. This small act of defiance made me feel as good as finally getting some outside time.

# CHAPTER 10

# Be Our Guest

*Mandeville, Louisiana, 2000*

Warm orange and yellows fell heavy on my eyelids, causing me to open my eyes to the morning. I blinked the sunlight through my lashes, reaching out to feel its warmth but to no avail. The coldness that penetrated my soul seemed so frozen that no matter how I tried, it was impenetrable. I took a deep breath and stepped out of bed, trying to find the positive by telling myself that I was ahead of the day by already being dressed, even though they were just the clothes I'd slept in for the last four days.

Lincoln's fingers gripped the edge of the crib in the corner of the room. He cheerfully called to me, "Momma!" his one-year-old speech slurred. My hope, my joy, my only reason for fighting each day, hours, and sometimes, even minutes. My children were my constant reminder that I had a purpose, that others needed me and that this suffering had to be endured, no matter what.

"Good morning, Linky!" I kissed his pillow-like cheek. I could softly hear the TV on before opening the bedroom door. Rachael and Alex were sitting side by side on the floor watching the movie *Balto*, both in a pair of Rachael's pajamas. Rachael had her blue Princess

Jasmine nightgown on, and Alex was wearing a pink nightgown with a kitten on the front and lace trim.

"Looking cute." I rubbed Alex's hair and walked into the kitchen.

"Mommy, I'm hungry," Alex called after me.

"All right, one second!"

I cut two big slices out of the chocolate cake on the counter and dropped the plate on the floor with two forks. Aside from the sugar, it was not a half-bad breakfast. There were eggs, flour, and milk in there. I bounced Lincoln in my arms as we watched Balto and his sled team of huskies race through the snow. Speaking of pets, where in the world was our cat? I looked out the kitchen window and saw our orange cat, Tiger, perched over the giant Tupperware container that doubled as our goldfish aquarium. He slid his tail back and forth across the pavement before standing on his hind legs and striking a fish out of the bucket. The shiny fish slapped against the cement and flopped around in the small puddle.

"Not again." I moaned as I set Lincoln in his high chair and opened the porch door. The fish was gone. Tiger walked to the door and weaved his furry body in between my legs, purring as if thanking me for buying Rachael fifteen goldfish for her birthday. We were now at seven goldfish and on a steady decline. The credits rolled on the TV in front of my kids' chocolate- frosted faces.

"Go put some real clothes on and then we can open Rachael's butterflies." I smiled.

Rachael's eyes got huge. "Yeah!" she and Alex screamed in unison before they took off running down the hall. Yep, I had also gotten Rachael a butterfly hatchery for her birthday. It was an animal-themed birthday, after all. The butterflies hatched last night before bed, so I told them we would play with them in the morning. And morning it was.

"We're dressed and ready!" Rachael chimed, sliding into the kitchen in her socks.

"We're ready, we're ready, we're reaaaadyyy!" Alex screamed, his four-year-old jumping-bean self bouncing out of control.

I opened the top cupboard where I had been hiding the container of butterflies and pulled it down. Instantly Rachael and Alex were like moths to a flame. They could not stop touching the plastic walls or peering inside as we all walked to the playroom.

I gripped the clasp to open the container. "Okay, you guys ready?"

"Yes!" they yelled, jumping. I do not think Alex ever stopped jumping. I released the clasp, and two monarch butterflies flew out, then another, and another, until the room danced in butterfly confetti. Two landed on Rachael's shirt and one on her face. Alex wasn't one to wait for them to land on him. He liked to chase them and catch them in his hands. I put a butterfly on my finger and brought it down to Lincoln.

"Look, so pretty." I held it in front of him, and he looked up at me, smiling.

The doorbell rang. Who could that be? I had invited the sister missionaries over for lunch, but it couldn't already be noon. I opened the front door, and sure enough, there were two girls in skirts with missionary name tags. The missionaries in our church taught people about Jesus Christ and the Book of Mormon while spending much of their day doing service in the community. Since missionaries lived on a budget and had limited time, members of our church usually invited them over for meals.

"Sisters, come in!" I welcomed, holding Lincoln on my hip.

"Good afternoon, Sister Wasden." They always cheerily smiled. "Shoes on or off?"

"Off please, you can just leave them by the door. Kids, come help set the table!"

Rachael and Alex came running into the kitchen with butterflies on their shirts.

"Mommy, look! All the butterflies are on us!" Alex shouted.

"Where did you get all those?" one of the missionaries asked.

"For my birthday. Want to hold one?" Rachael reached her hand out with a little monarch butterfly resting on it.

"Sure." She lifted her hand, forming a bridge that the butterfly could walk across. I, of course, had lost track of time and did not have the strength even to begin to attempt preparing something for lunch. Luckily, I had some shredded chicken warming in the oven for the kids. I realized I needed more than one course, so I set a bowl of popcorn on the table in front of the sisters next to a pan of cake batter I had not had a chance to bake.

"Thanks for lunch, Sister Wasden," the sisters kindly said as my kids started serving themselves a handful of popcorn and spoonfuls of cake batter as if this was their daily meal. The sisters watched them and awkwardly but politely spooned the batter on their plate and it soon pooled into their popcorn.

Pain started to fill my chest. It was not brought on by anything that I could figure out. It just came. Daily. The constant weight of darkness clung to me, and I could feel the recurring pain chugging through my veins with each heartbeat. It was that feeling when you know something painful is about to hit, and you will welcome anything to take the edge off. How many times had I talked to the cashiers at Wal-Mart telling them I was close, personal friends with Angelina Jolie, Tom Cruise, or Oprah, and needed to find them the perfect birthday present, then asked for their opinion on the gifts I had found? So, it was no surprise that I started looking for a distraction. I needed something to take me away from the emotional wave about to pull me under, and I needed to find it fast.

"Have you ever eaten cat?" I asked as Tiger jumped up on the table and sniffed Lincoln's tray of popcorn.

"No, I haven't," one of the sisters answered. She looked at Tiger walking across people's plates.

"Well, today will be a first then." The oven beeped, and I got up to check it. The sisters were quiet for a while, hoping I would clarify. But I let them linger in their uncertainty.

"Wait, are you cooking this cat?" one of them finally decided to ask.

"No, no." I laughed and pulled out a bowl of shredded chicken from the oven.

"Oh." The sisters looked at each other in relief and started laughing too.

"I cooked his brother." I placed the steaming hot pan right in front of them. "Ran over him this morning, which gave me plenty of time to skin him in preparation for our lunch." I ran my hands down my lap. "Now, who would like to say the blessing?" The sisters' faces went white.

"Me!" Alex stood on his chair. We all folded our arms, and Alex stayed standing while he prayed. "Dear heavenly father, thanks for the butterflies, and the yummy cake."

"And the cat," I chimed in.

"And the cat. Name of Jesus Christ, amen."

The sisters hesitantly spooned small piles of chicken onto their plates and looked at me before picking up their forks.

"Don't worry. You can start. I still have to dish the kids up," I encouraged, even though I knew etiquette was not the reason behind their hesitation. I served my kids, subtly watching the sisters slowly chew as they inspected every taste that hit their tongues. It probably didn't help that Tiger circled between our guests' feet while they tried not to focus on what they were eating.

I took the kids grocery shopping after the sisters left because clearly there was not much in the pantry. Alex and Rachael struggled to walk beside me through the aisles of Wal-Mart. Lincoln, my youngest, was standing in the grocery cart, wearing nothing but a diaper. Whenever I put a new item in the cart, he giggled and dropped on his bum and squished the food. I was too exhausted even to care. Only one more step and we were out of here. I successfully gathered my kids up and made it to the checkout line. I slipped the separation bar behind the person in front of me and began stacking boxes of mac and cheese on the conveyer belt. Rachael decided to copy me, but rather than stacking mac and cheese, she heaped Hershey bars.

"No, Rachael, we're not buying those," I said, stuffing them back in the cardboard box.

Alex then decided to try Rachael's technique but with different candy, Push Pops, which encouraged Rachael to try again. Every time I turned around, there were little mounds of candy slapped onto the conveyer belt. Lincoln started clapping and stomping the bread under his bare feet.

"Guys, please stop." I turned back to the cart and took the bread from under Lincoln. It was completely flattened. The cashier scanned it. "Great," I whispered to myself. I tossed up the rest of the groceries and got out my wallet. Then I looked down and saw Rachael and Alex sitting on the floor with a pile of candy spread on the ground.

"Please put the candy back!" I pleaded, looking at the line of people.

The cashier glanced up at me, and I forced a smile. She continued scanning items as I tapped my credit card on the counter. I felt like a disorganized mom on display for the line of people behind me. They were definitely judging me, but I hoped I was just being paranoid.

"Um, Mama?" Alex said as he pointed to Lincoln.

"Yeah?" I looked up and saw Lincoln standing with his diaper in one hand as he stood peeing over the side of the cart.

"We need a custodian to come to cashier number four," the cashier spoke into the intercom. The speaker clicked off, and I looked back at the cashier. I swiped my credit card and signed before the custodian wheeled a mop through the line. Humiliated and embarrassed, I grabbed some paper towels from the custodian's cart.

"Don't worry. I'll clean it up." I got down on my knees and began wiping down the floor and threw the paper towels in his trash can. He proceeded to sanitize the area.

"Mommy, I'm thirsty," Rachael complained. I couldn't take any more, so I stood up and grabbed a water bottle out of the refrigerated display by the checkout line.

"Hey, can I just quickly buy this?" I pleaded with the cashier.

"No, you'll have to go to the back of the line." She pointed to the long line of people waiting to check out.

"Are you kidding?" I widened my eyes.

Showing not an ounce of mercy, she reiterated, "Please go to the back of the line." The cashier got ready for the person behind me. I looked down at the line of people, then back at my diaperless kid.

I already felt emotionally disturbed every day of my life. So, this was as good a time as any to sin. I opened the water bottle, smiled at the cashier and the people in line, then raised the water like I was toasting them and took a big swallow.

"Mommy, it's a sin to steal," Alex said, pulling on my shirt to get my attention.

"Yep, it is, Alex. We will repent later. Here's your water, Rachael." I held out the bottle to her.

"No, Mommy, that's sinful water," Rachael insisted.

"I'm telling Dad what you did," Alex said.

I rolled my eyes and continued to walk right out the doors without paying. A range of emotions ran through my body. In a moment of impulsiveness, I yelled as loud as I could, "I'm shoplifting, arrest me!"

I then pushed my grocery cart full of smashed groceries, a naked child, and two other kids in tow, out the big double doors of Wal-Mart. Living everyday life had become increasingly hard for me, even when my situations weren't difficult. Having people over for lunch or the basic task of grocery shopping pushed me over the edge.

As I looked back on my life, I asked the same question I had pondered for thirteen years: "God, why am I in so much pain?" Was I a sinner? Was this some kind of divine biblical punishment? Was it because I was not a good enough person, student, mom, church member, wife, sister, or friend? And most importantly, did God not care about me? Why did he not answer my prayers? Was I not worth saving? Those questions hit my heart with a resounding answer that I had to accept. Apparently, God was in no rush to help me, so I was going to save myself.

# CHAPTER 11

# Psych Ward

*Day Three, Evening*

Visiting hours were finally here, and I stood as close to the entrance doors as the guards would let me. Each time they looked away, I inched myself closer. Occasionally the doors would open, and a visitor would come in. Each time the metal bar pushed open I stood a little taller, thinking this time it had to be Mitch, but the longer I didn't see him, the more I thought he was not coming. Maybe our fights were worse than I realized, and he had decided to throw in the towel. The days had become so predictable: there was the morning fight, the afternoon fight on the phone while Mitch was at work, and the evening fight when he got home. It seemed like fighting made up most of our relationship.

The massive doors pushed open one last time, and there he stood. Mitch, my everything, my rock. I ran into his arms and felt instantly safe. It was the only time I felt safe in that place. He tried to let go, but I wouldn't let him. I needed a few more minutes.

"Sonja, let's sit down." He grinned. "How are you feeling?"

"Take me home with you." I hugged him tighter.

"You'll be home soon." He walked us to the nearest couch and plopped his head on top of mine, exhausted. In silence, we stayed glued in that position, enjoying not being separated. With my head on his shoulder, I wondered what the next steps would be. I was in a hospital that Mitch thought was supposed to help us solve something, but there was no guarantee that would happen. After a while, I looked up at him. "What's going to happen to us?"

"I don't know." He combed his fingers through my hair. "But we'll be okay." He rested his head back on mine, and I wanted to believe him.

"Visiting hours are over," a nurse came from the front desk to inform us. Mitch kissed me, and I watched him walk out. He turned and waved to me as the massive doors slowly shut, and I was alone again.

CHAPTER 12

# A Date with Destiny, Tony Robbins

*Tampa, Florida, 2000*

I was just like any other heavy person trying to lose weight. I tried every program under the sun but kept getting heavier. I had bought Tony Robbins's tapes on Neuro-Linguistic Programming (NLP), which was supposed to help me associate pain with overeating rather than pleasure. But listening to his tapes for hours while cleaning didn't make much of a dent in my weight. I finished Tony's program but still carried all the baggage that emotional pain and cellulite had to offer. I decided that I needed Tony Robbins himself. Admittedly, I was missing something key, or perhaps I needed specialized advice not found in his audiobooks, the kind of information his famous clients had access to. But there was one big problem: people paid him millions of dollars to help them, and I did not have a million dollars.

At 3 A.M. I slowly slid out of bed, trying not to make a sound. Mitch was a light sleeper, and I didn't want to reveal my latest plan to win my battle with overeating. My toes made it to the floor, and I cautiously pulled my packed bag from under the bed. To prevent my bag from hitting something in the dark, I held it close to my stomach, which bulged out over my elastic band skirt. I took one step toward the door and the floorboards creaked.

"Sonja, what are you doing?" Mitch squinted in the dark.

I froze. Mitch sleepily walked up behind me and looked at my bag pressed against my chest. I carefully turned around to face him, wishing I could hide the evidence of my travel plans, and say I was just getting a drink.

"Are you leaving me?" He creased his eyebrows and took the bag out of my arms.

"No! Of course not. I left a note by the bed."

"Then what's this?" He lifted the bag in the air.

"I can explain." I looked over at the red numbers glowing on our nightstand. "But I have to explain fast because I still need to buy a ticket at the airport."

"Where are you going at three in the morning?" He was fully awake now.

"Tony Robbins is going to be at the QVC home shopping network headquarters in Pennsylvania to sell his personal power program. I need to convince the QVC people to let me talk to him. Mitch, he can help me!"

Mitch seemed to be trying to figure out if he was still asleep or if I had really said something crazy. "Sonja, you're scaring me." He sat down at the edge of the bed and ran his fingers through the top of his hair. "The QVC people are not going to let you in to talk to Tony Robbins."

"I'll find a way. If I have to wait outside all day until he comes out, I will. He's the only person who can help me."

"And why would he help a stranger waiting on the street?"

"He has a big heart."

Mitch put his hand over his forehead. "Sonja, he's there to sell a product, not give you a free coaching session. Tony Robbins is famous. If you show up stalking him unannounced, they'll call security on you, or worse, arrest you."

"It just seems like he cares about people when he talks on his tapes," I countered.

"He has thousands of people begging for his help. It won't work."

"I have to go! Please, Mitch, this is my big chance." I picked my bag up from the ground.

"This is extreme and impulsive behavior. Sonja, I can't let you go."

I missed my plane that morning, but I wasn't sad. I knew I was going to meet Tony Robbins. I would just have to wait for Mitch to get out of the way.

A few hours later, Mitch kissed me on his way out to work. I pretended to lie sleepily in bed. As soon as the door closed, I jumped out of bed. Tony had live seminars all over the country. I just had to pay and go to one. But how to get his attention, that was the question. I knew he was going to be at the QVC headquarters. That was my answer! I dialed the number in West Chester, Pennsylvania.

"Hi, this is Sonja Wasden. I'm going to be working with Tony Robbins at his Date with Destiny seminar coming up and I forgot to mail him important documents." I was not above white lies to achieve my goals. After all, I was going to be working with him, so that wasn't a complete lie. He just didn't know it yet.

"Wait. What's your name again?"

"Sonja Wasden. Look, these documents need to be in Tony's hands by tomorrow. I know he's going to be there to promote his Personal Power Program. Would you be kind enough to give it to him?"

"Um." The woman on the line hesitated.

"This is crucial. Tony has to have these documents in his hands tomorrow, or I'm in trouble. I can FedEx them to you personally, and then you can see that there are only documents inside. Will you help me?"

"I guess I can do that."

"Promise me you won't forget. It's important."

"I'll make sure Tony gets them," she promised.

Freedom was finally within my grasp. I spent hours writing and editing my letter hoping to convince Tony Robbins to help me. I stepped away from the FedEx counter after mailing my letter to QVC headquarters believing I was finally on my way to overcoming my obsession with food.

After much debate, Mitch and I came to an agreement that I would go to the Date with Destiny seminar in Florida. After the plane landed in Tampa, I yanked my duffle bag from under the seat in front of me. Today was the day I would find out if my letter had worked.

As I entered the auditorium an overwhelming amount of energy vibrated within the room. Music played loudly as smoke floated off the sides of the stage while the dancers moved under the flashing lights. Two massive flat-screen TVs showed people skiing off cliffs and motorbiking. The room was filled with hundreds of people. Timidly, I looked at my ticket and walked to my preassigned seat.

"Have you ever been to one of these before?" the woman next to me asked.

"No, this is my first time."

At that moment I felt shy. I wasn't dancing or screaming. I just clapped my hands together and watched the frenzy. A short man in a suit walked out into the energetic chaos.

"Give it up for Tony Robbins!" his voice rang through the microphone. Music blasted, and Tony Robbins came running out the side entrance, forcefully clapping his hands together. The audience lost their minds.

"There he is!" the women next to me elbowed my arm and screamed. I smiled. The music faded out, and Tony adjusted his microphone.

"Thank you for that kind introduction," he said, facing the announcer. "And thank you for being here at Date with Destiny!" He cheered into the microphone, and the crowd cheered with him. The woman next to me was very good at this whole screaming thing. "Now, I received a letter." Tony reached into his pocket and held up my letter. I was stunned. I guess I was hoping it would happen, but not this soon and not publicly. I was hoping we could talk privately. He held the letter high above his head.

"What have I done," I whispered to myself. Realizing my plan had worked made me excited and terrified all at the same time, but mostly terrified.

"Dear Tony, I'm writing to you because I think you're my last chance at being helped," he read to the crowd.

My neck and cheeks burned with embarrassment. I had reread and edited that letter so many times I knew exactly what was coming next. I cringed in my seat before he got to the extremely personal parts. Listening to the audience's reactions to parts of the letter made me wish I hadn't been so descriptive. I wasn't sure I could match my face with the person who wrote all those things he had just read. But I would never see these people again, and I had to be brave. I had gotten this far, after all. On his tapes, Tony told numerous stories about how he had changed people's lives in his seminars. My heart beat with nervous excitement at the thought of being one of his miracle stories.

He was finally getting to the end of the letter: "I've gained a lot of weight and can't stop eating." Tony widened his eyes and looked out at the crowd. He brought his arms forward in a circle to make himself look fat and continued reading: "I need to get my eating under control."

The crowd burst into laughter, and I hugged my stomach tight and pressed myself into the back of my chair. Any hope I had left of Tony Robbins curing me vanished. The hard truth hit me. He was making fun of me. Maybe I had set myself up to be publicly humiliated, but that did not change the fact that I was embarrassed. Then I had a realization. Part of Neuro-Linguistics Programming (NLP) was to create pain around what you don't want and pleasure around what you do want. So, of course he was trying to help me by linking pain to overeating.

"Whoever wrote this letter, stand up!" Tony pumped his arms, encouraging the crowd to cheer. Music began to play for my introduction.

I froze. I couldn't stand, especially not in front of all those people. I kept telling myself I would never see these people again, and maybe this was the price to pay for being cured. My sweaty palms gripped the sides of my chair. I wasn't sure if that was to keep me in my seat or to prepare me to get out of it, but either way, I sat frozen.

He looked at the bottom of the letter for my name. "Sonja! Stand up!" The music played its entire loop again as I sat in my chair. The longer I waited, the more embarrassing it felt to stand up. My heart sunk to the bottom of my shoes. Tears slowly streamed down my face. I could not do it.

He shrugged his shoulders. "Oh well," he said, and he moved on.

On my way back to my hotel, a thought came crashing down on me. I had come all this way for help, and I might go home without any. I was sure that Tony making fun of me was part of the therapy, and I had let my opportunity pass right by me. I took my duffle bag and filled it with all my junk food—chips, candy, and chocolate. I zipped it up and frantically pressed the elevator button down to the lobby.

"Deliver this to Tony Robbins's room." I tossed my bag up onto the front desk. The man in a green uniform eyed the bag and reached for it. "Wait!" I grabbed a pen off the counter and scribbled down my message for Tony on a piece of paper from a hotel notepad.

*Here's my food. I'm ready. –Sonja*

# CHAPTER 13

# Psych Ward

*Day Four*

Sydney and I walked to the conference room filled with people. I took an empty seat and waited to hear what the sudden meeting was for.

"Someone in this room is stealing the crayons, and it needs to stop!" Jane looked out at the sea of patients. "Tell me who it is, and we will restock the crayons."

I looked side to side to see if anyone would fess up. Everyone knew someone was stealing the crayons at the drawing table. First, all the blue crayons went, then red, and then green. The theft caused some of the patients to lose their cool when trying to color. People complained that only brown and orange crayons were left. Today the browns got stolen.

"Who is the thief?" Jane demanded.

A young man sitting behind me started giggling, and another patient to my right joined in. Jane pointed to each one of them. "Are you the thieves?"

They giggled harder and nodded their heads.

"Stop laughing," she scolded them, which only made them laugh harder. "This is not funny. Give me the stolen crayons!"

A patient from behind me shot up her hand, laughing. "It's me, I stole them!"

"No, I'm the crayon thief!" another patient confessed.

"You four go to your rooms!" Jane yelled over the laughter.

They got up and left, laughing the whole way to their rooms. I felt laughter surfacing in my chest. I put my hand over my mouth to stop it.

A man in the front jumped up. "After my little stint here, I'm going to jail, so I might as well confess, I stole them!"

More and more of us started laughing, and Jane kept dismissing people to their rooms as they confessed to stealing the crayons. There ended up just being three of us left who had not confessed. I was proud I made it to the final three. But in the end, I couldn't control myself and burst out laughing too. I was immediately dismissed to my room. Sydney and I sat on our beds.

"Who do you think stole the crayons?" I asked.

"Maybe it was Jane," Sydney suggested.

"I swear this place is just like an elementary school. But you teach at one, so what do you think?"

"Yeah, this place isn't so different, makes me feel right at home," she said sarcastically.

"Do you like being a schoolteacher?" I asked.

"Yeah, I do."

"I bet you're good at it."

"I have this treasure box filled with stickers and little toys that the kids can purchase with golden bucks that they earn for good behavior. It's fun." She smiled.

"I bet they miss you."

"Do you like being a mom?" Sydney asked.

"I love it. I miss my kids so much." My heart was breaking. I hated that the hospital did not allow children to visit even if they knew their parent's situation, and mine did. I would say I didn't believe in putting up facades for children, but the truth was, I didn't know how to. My kids understood with an abnormal amount of clarity what I was experiencing.

"What are they like?" she asked.

A nurse interrupted before I could answer. "Sonja, it's time for you to meet with Dr. Barry."

"Again?" I reluctantly sighed.

"Yes, you meet with him once a day, you already know that," she quipped impatiently. I quietly followed her to the room where Dr. Barry was sitting. I think the nurses did that to make sure we didn't skip appointments, although it's not like we had much else going on in here.

"Good afternoon." Dr. Barry straightened his white coat. I sat down and managed to send a forced smile in his direction while I braced myself for more questions.

"Would you say you're impulsive?" He clicked his pen, ready to write down a list of crazy behavior, no doubt.

"No," I answered, hoping to disappoint him.

"So, it says here that you and the kids were late to church but you decided you just had to pull into a car wash and power wash your car."

"So what? It was filthy. I didn't want to be that family that drives to church in a car that's so dirty kids write 'wash me' on the windows."

"But it says here, after washing the outside, you power washed the inside of the van too. Does that strike you as impulsive?"

"Not really."

"Did it destroy the van?"

"Well . . . yeah," I admitted awkwardly. "I didn't realize that much water would rot all the electrical wiring and seat fabric. It lasted about a week after that." I hoped he would see the situation for what it was—an honest mistake—and not some radical behavior. "Look, I see you're reading the notes my dad gave you. It's not all what you think."

"What about losing eighty thousand dollars playing the stock market?"

"Lots of people lose money in the stock market."

"True. But you bought and sold like you were playing blackjack in Vegas."

"I don't want to talk about this."

"Okay. It also says here that you gained and then lost over one hundred pounds." His eyes widened. "When did you start gaining weight?"

"After I had my third baby, I started eating a lot."

"What caused your eating habits to change so dramatically?"

"An extreme case of baby blues is what my doctor said. But I didn't gain a hundred pounds overnight. It happened one candy bar at a time," I said, thinking back on my old habits. "I used to eat all my kids' Halloween candy, but I always bought more before they got home to replace it. It was on sale the day after Halloween anyway."

"Would your kids get upset?"

"No, they were used to it. Whenever we had any desserts in the house, my kids would beg me to save them a piece for after school. Of course, when they got home, I would have eaten the whole thing. So we would all drive to the store and buy another one. No big deal."

"How do you think that affected your children?"

"It didn't affect them," I said, finding the question offensive.

"Sonja, there's no way your children haven't been affected by your illness."

"First, I'm not ill. Second, I would protect my children at all costs, even from myself!"

"I don't doubt that. But all parents harm their kids in some way, even if we don't want to see it." Dr. Barry's comment stung as I considered the possibility of his statement.

# CHAPTER 14

---

# A Date with Destiny,
# Tony Robbins

*Part Two*

That night Tony brought up my bag of junk food and dumped it all out on the stage.

"'Here's my food. I'm ready. Sonja.'" He read off the note. "Well, Sonja, come on up!"

The music started up again. It was a tune I was getting to know all too well. This was it, Tony was going to perform NLP on me, and I would be cured of my overeating.

The women sitting next to me stared as I started my walk down the aisle. The crowd of people stood clapping, scanning the room, looking for the person—me—who wrote the note. I could feel my face getting warm. The spotlight following me up the steps was not helping. I made it to the stage and stood next to a smiling Tony Robbins.

"Sonja, you've gained an incredible amount of weight. What do you think is causing it?" Tony asked in a strong voice.

"Well, I don't know if I would call it incredible," I replied. The crowd hummed a soft chuckle. I looked out at the audience, but the lights kept most of the crowd from being very visible. "But I would say I eat because it fills me up in a way that life can't."

"What I'm hearing is you've turned to food because you lack something. There's an essential need you have, but it's not being filled, so you eat. Would you say that's correct?" Tony looked directly into my eyes as we stood on display under the blinding lights.

I held on to my jean overalls for some sense of stability as I processed his question and responded, "Yes," into the microphone.

"Do you know what you're missing in life that food temporarily fills for you?" Tony asked.

"I'm not sure. Maybe comfort, maybe a small piece of enjoyment?" My hands slightly shook, and Tony turned back to the audience.

"When we lack something, the obvious reaction is to fill it with something. The problem is, we usually don't spend enough time investigating our need before we choose something to fill it with." He paused and looked back at me. "So while you may say you don't know what you're lacking, I have to wonder, from reading your letter, if your problem might stem from your relationship with your father."

The crowd started cheering before I could say anything. I was ushered off the stage. My dad? I didn't see how my eating and my dad were correlated. Tony's answer left me confused. It made me wonder if I hadn't examined my relationship with my dad correctly and did that play a part in my overeating? I stayed for the rest of the conference and used the techniques of NLP to consciously link pain to the idea of overeating and pleasure to the idea of being thin and healthy. I began living Tony's mantra of "Nothing tastes as good as thin feels!"

The process made an impact and I lost weight. I thought that losing the weight would lift my emotional pain, but even as the weight came off, the emotional pain remained. As the stresses of my life increased, I seemed less capable of following the helpful steps Tony had taught me and gained all the weight back and even more. I knew what Tony did helped millions of people, but my problems seemed to run deeper than the average person's. It was only treating my symptoms, like giving a cancer patient an energy drink because they felt fatigued. Something else was stopping my progress but I couldn't figure out what. I was not convinced that my relationship with my dad was the root cause of my pain. But if not that, then what?

# CHAPTER 15

# Psych Ward

*Day Five*

Brent was sitting at a table with his head down, drawing on a piece of paper. It was already three in the afternoon, and I had just woken up from my medicated slumber.

"Do you want to tell me some more historical facts?" I asked, taking the seat next to him.

"No," he solemnly replied.

"You really should go on *Jeopardy*. You would win."

Brent lifted his head slightly. "I-I-I have th-thought about it." I think most people ignored him because he had a hard time speaking; his stutter could make it hard to understand him, but he was truly a genius. I could ask him about any event in history, and he knew the month, day, and year it happened.

"What are you drawing?" I looked at the upside-down picture.

"Th-th-is is you." He pointed to the rose he had colored. "Th-th-is is me." He moved his finger down to the weeds.

"No. It's not, Brent." I took his paper and drew a daisy next to the rose. "That's you. We're all just different flowers." Brent looked at the addition to his picture and traced his finger over the daisy.

"Wait out here until dinner starts," Jane said to a new patient. Jane looked like a thick tree stump next to the tall, lean woman. The new patient had cranberry hair and a disapproving scowl. She sat down at the table across from me. I noticed her arms were covered in razor cuts. I stared at her arms, amazed at how many scars she left out in the open.

"What?" she demanded.

Startled, I looked away. "Oh, nothing."

I understood cutting, but cutting and letting the whole world see it, that was brave. I continued to sneak glances at her. To me, she was no different than a soldier bearing the marks of battle. She didn't hide the evidence of past pain. I wondered what that kind of openness felt like but never planned on trying it out.

Sydney had her therapy appointment after dinner, so I ate fast and went to my room, hoping to have some alone time. I lay across the bed, looking up at the ceiling. A soft tapping on my door echoed through the room. I pulled my feet into some socks and opened the door. A small nun smiled at me; the loose skin around her eyes wrinkled. I had seen her throughout the week meeting with patients, so I supposed tonight was my turn.

"I'm Sister Murray. May we sit in the conference area and talk?" Her gentle voice matched her sweet, frail frame.

"Of course." I followed her to a couch and sat on the edge as her small hands held a Bible to her chest.

"Are there any questions you'd like to ask me?"

I didn't plan on having any questions, but her presence was so intrinsically safe, I wanted her to help me.

"Well, I do have a somewhat religious question," I admitted.

She nodded and smiled, encouraging me to continue.

"I go to church every week, read my scriptures and pray, yet I feel all the punishment of a sinner."

"What do you mean by punishment?"

"You know in the Bible where it talks about the weeping, gnashing of teeth, and being cast out into outer darkness?"

"Yes."

"That's how I feel inside. I feel like I'm in outer darkness."

"Do you feel guilty about any unresolved sins?" Sister Murray asked.

"We are all sinners, as you know, but I've thought about that a lot and always concluded that I hadn't committed any big sins. I've prayed a thousand prayers and begged for forgiveness and peace. I'm not sure what I lack, but I don't understand how I can feel everything the scriptures say about being a damned soul in hell, and not be evil."

"Never think you're evil. You may just have strong emotions running through you." She put her hand over mine.

"If there were two groups of people, and one group had all the accomplished, righteous, lovely people and the other group had the drug addicts, prostitutes, and broken souls, I would belong with the broken souls."

Sister Murray opened her Bible and read me a passage from Colossians 3. "Let the peace of Christ rule in your hearts since as members of one body you were called to peace. And be thankful." She left me with a prayer. It was sweet, but my question was still unanswered. I went to my room and hid under the covers, wishing I could disappear from the earth, but since my children needed me, I remained.

# CHAPTER 16

# Falling Behind

*Sugar Land, Texas, 2002*

I sat across the table from the principal and my daughter's teacher. Rachael was in third grade and just diagnosed with dyslexia. Finally, they knew why she was having trouble learning to read. I felt such a huge relief. I had tried everything, and it seemed like she made very little progress. She could only read at a kindergarten level.

"Your daughter's going to have to repeat third grade. There's no possible way she can catch up," the principal informed me.

The words "my daughter" and "no possible way" caught my attention.

"Of course she can," I replied, full of confidence.

"While I appreciate your enthusiasm, you have to understand there's just no way she'll pass the state test in April," he assured me.

"Don't worry, she'll pass." I smiled.

Thinking he had to help this poor delusional woman, he got out a piece of paper and drew a stick person representing Rachael and put other stick people far ahead of her, representing the other students. He then drew lines showing improvement happening on both sides at the same speed. Since Rachael's line was farther back than everyone else's, it didn't matter that she was improving because the other students were improving too, so they were always ahead of her.

"She can't make up that much ground. Even if she progresses, the other kids will be progressing too, and she'll always be the one behind." The principal pointed to the paper.

"I see what you're trying to say, but she will go on to fourth grade. She'll catch up. There's always a way, and I'll find it," I insisted.

"Mrs. Wasden, in all my twenty-five years of being a teacher and principal, when a child is this far behind, they never catch up."

"No! We're—"

"She. Will. Never. Catch. Up."

"Thank you for your advice, but I guess you'll just have to wait and see," I told him.

He stood his ground. "No, Mrs. Wasden, I won't."

I stood up, not convinced, and he followed my lead and stood up too. I held out my hand, and he shook it. I walked out his office door, committed to getting Rachael up to grade level. I had full faith in my daughter and her ability. I was angry at the principal's attitude. It was no wonder students did not reach their full potential in schools if the schools themselves didn't believe in the students. I was fully prepared to teach him a lesson that he would never forget. Faith. Belief. Hard Work. These were miracle workers.

We finally knew what was wrong. Rachael was dyslexic. Now we just had to work at it. I had seven months to catch her up before the state test. Dyslexia wasn't the only obstacle we were facing. I had not showered or changed my clothes in two weeks. The pain and exhaustion inside me burned so hotly that I thought some nights I was literally dying. Life felt like I was crawling on broken glass just to take care of my kids' basic needs. But I dug even deeper, giving more of myself to save my daughter from falling behind.

I visited THINKERS, a specialized program for children with dyslexia, severe auditory processing deficiency, poor memory skills, or exhibit poor retention. I paid for every course they suggested for Rachael and then some. We also bought all the take-home programs. A teacher named Effie worked primarily with Rachael on a cognitive enhancement program called PACE, which was often referred to as "Mental Boot Camp." The PACE program was designed for students like Rachael who had extreme difficulty keeping up with their peers. Rachael spent two hours every day in Effie's office reading, writing, and working on her auditory analysis and processing speed. She would call out words and have her spell out the sounds, even nonsense words like "gr" or "eck." These programs allowed Rachael to make significant progress in a short period of time.

After tutoring with Effie at THINKERS, Rachael did an extra hour with a teacher named Suzanne, a blond woman in her forties who loved to cook and shared treats with the kids. We went to her home, and she would break words apart and have Rachael practice using them in sentences. She cut dozens of words in half and then called out a word for Rachael to try and spell by piecing together letters from two piles of paper.

Every morning before school Rachael and I studied for an hour while she sat on my bed with her perfectly gelled pigtails and ate her breakfast. We went over the never-ending pile of flash cards.

By the end of all the tutoring, Rachel and I were worn out, but we still had the homework to finish from her teachers at school. Many nights I would find her asleep at the kitchen table with her little cheek lying on her big textbook. Mitch always carried her to bed. For the next seven months, we continued this rigorous study schedule.

The day of the state test, I knelt with her, and we said a prayer. "Our Heavenly Father, Rachael and I have done everything we could do. Please send angels to help her as she takes this test. In the name of Jesus Christ, amen." We got up from our knees and hugged.

"It's in God's hands now," I quietly and calmly told her.

The day of the test I lay in bed and prayed. I had been running on fumes, and I collapsed at the finish line. At times like this, Mitch had to drag me into the bathtub and bathe me. He'd run the water until I was ready to go in and then scrub my body and wash my hair. Over the years he would do this hundreds of times. I also couldn't brush my teeth. The task seemed too enormous. He would bring a toothbrush and a cup of water to the bed and brush my teeth for me. These simple tasks of daily living felt like climbing an insurmountable mountain and I literally could not do them. All my energy was channeled toward the kids. Mitch's kindness, strength, patience, and love fed my bottomless soul. We were a team in every sense of the word, but he was also emotionally running on fumes. The reason I had any energy at all for my children was that, in many ways, I was drawing it from my husband.

I took my kids to lessons like any typical mother. However, I didn't look like every other mother. I had stains all over my clothes, which I hadn't changed in weeks. Mitch knew not to bring up things like changing my clothes or an epic argument would ensue. I liked my clothes and the comfort that wearing the same thing each day brought me. I could not stand the change of putting on new clothes, and it just didn't seem like a good place to spend the limited energy I had.

A friend of Alex's asked me one day, "Why don't you change your clothes?"

"I do," I lied. "I just buy six of the same shirt and skirts." That part was true.

"Then why are there the same dirty spots on all of them?" He had me. Leave it to kids to tell the bold truth.

"I don't know." What else could I say?

"My mom counts the number of days you wear the same outfit. She said you're on day seven," he informed me.

It felt like someone had punched me in the stomach. I didn't want to face the fact that people noticed my struggles. I'm sure the grease in my hair could also not be missed. I just always told myself it looked like I had gel in my hair, another lie.

You would think that with the information that people did notice, I would start to at least change my clothes. I did not. It was just too much work. I had to save every ounce of energy for my kids. So, I would sacrifice what other people thought of me. It had to be done. I could not let my kids down. That would be the ultimate blow. I pretended that no one could see that there was anything wrong with me. I was fine. I was the fun mom who planned museum trips, zoo sleepovers, swim parties, and other activities for my kids and the neighborhood. I went as far as claiming we were a homeschooling group (which we were not) to get the Houston Zoo to bring their Zoo Mobile, full of live animals, to one of our swim parties.

At the time, I would tell myself that lots of people didn't shower for weeks on end and did not change their clothes. Even if most of them were homeless, they were still people.

Several weeks later I got a call from the principal. "Mrs. Wasden, I got the state test results and looked at Rachael's first."

I gripped the phone tighter.

"I believe an apology is in order. She passed."

Silence. Then it registered in my brain what he had said. She had passed. We had done it!

"Thank you! Thank you so much for calling and letting us know!" I was screaming with excitement and quickly hung up the phone.

I picked Rachael up from school that day, and her teacher was crying. No one could believe she had passed. That day Rachael learned she could overcome difficult trials, but what kind of example was I?

I taught my children that with God, all things are possible. Did I really believe that? I did for other people, but for myself, truthfully, I doubted it. I was hanging on by a thread that could snap at any moment. Where was my God? Why would he not help me out of this darkness? I was doing everything I knew: I went to doctors, kept trying different pills. Yet, I couldn't overcome this darkness and started believing it might not even be possible.

# CHAPTER 17

# Psych Ward

*Day Six*

S onja!" Jane stood in the doorway to my room.

"Yeah?" I looked up.

"Come to class," she demanded.

"I can't make it to class." I sat on my bed, feeling the morning meds hitting me like a freight train. Heavy sleep began to draw the curtains inside my head.

"Come to class now! The quicker you learn how to cooperate with us, the quicker you'll go home," Jane firmly replied.

The word "home" caught my attention. "I'll try." I stumbled to the conference room and hoped a small fraction of Jane's humane side would take pity on me.

"Okay, let's begin." Jane looked at a man in the front row with multiple tattoos up his arms. He seemed wide awake. I wondered if they were giving him any meds. If so, you would never know it.

"Why are you here?" Jane boldly asked him.

"I partied on my birthday and took some sleeping pills to sleep off the other drugs and alcohol. But my sister saw me dead asleep next to an open pill bottle. She thought I tried to kill myself and called 911. She totally misread the situation, but it's getting worked out."

"What have you learned from being here?"

"Nothing." He picked at his fingernails.

"I said, what have you learned?" Jane pursed her lips, but he was just as stubborn as she was.

He leaned back in his chair and sighed. "I told you, nothing." He then stared straight into her eyes; it was clear Jane felt she no longer had the power in the room. She squirmed under his gaze and straightened up.

"If you don't tell me what you've learned, I'm not letting you out of here. I have the power to do that, you know." Jane's threat fell flat.

The man got up and left the room.

Another patient soon followed him out, but before going, turned around and flipped Jane off. Jane quickly ignored the situation and began talking to the rest of the patients. I stood in the corner of the room shaking, trying to keep myself awake.

"There was a needle left in my room," another patient informed Jane.

"No, there was not. You imagined it."

"There really is a needle in my room. I think a nurse left it by accident," he insisted.

"You have to trust me. Your disease, your schizophrenia, is playing games with your mind. There is no needle there." She brushed him off.

I wondered why she wouldn't go look in his room, just to make sure. There could be a needle in his room left from his roommate's daily shots.

"Just because he has schizophrenia doesn't mean he imagines everything." I heard my voice fall into the center of the room before I realized I was speaking.

"Sonja. What is wrong with you? Are you having a panic attack?" Jane peered over at me shaking in the corner.

"No, I'm trying" —my eyelids continued to fall even though I was only halfway through my sentence— "to keep myself awake."

"Good. Keep doing that," she replied in an approving tone.

I wanted to scream and tell her to take some of my medicine, and then I would sit there and tell her to come to class and stay awake. What was wrong with her? She was obviously in the wrong profession.

"Forget it." I walked out and headed straight for my room. I was not about to disgrace myself once again and have the nurses carry me to my bed. I was an adult and could do that myself. On my way to my room, I saw Brent running down the hall.

"Brent?" I called after him.

He blazed past me in a full sprint. "I'm going to light myself on fiiiiiiiirrrrrrrrre!" he screamed. Two men quickly restrained him and pushed a needle in his arm. He fell limp, and they dragged him to his room. My eyelids dropped again, and I knew I was about to get knocked out by my medication. I pushed the door to my room open and collapsed on the bed. As I fell into a sleepy haze, I kept thinking about Brent being dragged across the brown tile. He and I weren't so different. I felt I could lose it that same way at any given moment.

My sister Allyson walked in during visiting hours and hugged me. "Surprise, lucky lady!"

"Allyson! What are you doing here?" I looked up at my mini-me. Allyson and I had matching black hair, light skin, and green eyes, but the weirdest similarity we shared was our voice. Whenever she called, my kids thought I was on the phone. Even though we looked similar, our personalities were entirely different. My mother always referred to her as the peacemaker, whereas I was the person disrupting the peace.

"I came down the day after you were admitted to help mom with your kids." She untied the belt around her cranberry red raincoat, gripped it like a lasso, and swung it into her other hand. "So, when do I get to break you out of here? I'm sure you've been keeping track of the nurses' rounds." I broke out in laughter.

"I can't tell you how happy I am that you're here." I hugged her back.

Even though Allyson was younger than me, she was emotionally stronger. When I was nine years old and she was six, we waited in our room for our dad to come spank us for one of our many childhood transgressions. I started crying before he even came to our room, but Allyson was laughing. She told me to laugh through the spanking because that made it hurt less, but I could never get myself to do it. I sobbed before, during, and after the discipline.

When Allyson was in law school, I went to her apartment, and it was a complete mess. She was lying in her pj's on the couch at noon. I asked what she was doing. Her response was, "Just sitting here thinking how great I am." Let me clarify that she never said these things sarcastically; she really believed what she said. Allyson was not arrogant, just beautifully confident. Not even in high school, when she was overweight, would bullying affect her. Because of her dark hair and light skin, kids called her Shamu, but she told me guys were intimidated by her intelligence and that's why she didn't get asked out. So of course, her boyfriend ended up being one of the most popular guys in high school. It was like her positive attitude willed good things to happen to her, and she ignored any negativity as merely background noise. I loved that about her.

"How are the kids?" I asked, sitting back down.

"They're good. Excited for you to come home, but good."

"And Mitch?"

"He's been strong. I did notice that your house is a mess, but all your pillowcases are ironed." She smiled and raised an eyebrow.

"I have my priorities straight."

"Clearly!" She laughed. Then the seriousness of my situation swallowed up her laughter, and we sat together in heavy silence.

"Allyson, what am I supposed to do when I get out of here? I want a guarantee that I won't get sent right back."

"Sonja"—she placed her hand on mine—"I don't know anyone more capable of hard things than you. When you get out of here, you're going to continue being the amazing mom and wife you are, but you also need to take care of yourself."

"But it feels like I only have enough in me to take care of my kids."

"I know. But you're going to get to a point where you can do both," she encouraged.

"What would I do without you?" I squeezed her hand.

"You don't need to worry about that. I'll always be here for you."

Despite our epic fights growing up, Allyson and I had developed a friendship that no number of unshared clothes or Scotch tape room dividers could sever. We had become each other's refuge. She was and still is the person I can say anything to. As we hugged goodbye and I watched her walk out the doors, I knew more than ever that I could not make it through this life without her.

# CHAPTER 18

# Hungry

*Sugar Land, Texas, 2002*

The consistently warm Texas sun felt good against my face. I wore my traditional long black skirt and a white T-shirt. My hair was pulled up in a greasy bun with two or three scrunchies and multiple pens shoved in it.

My feet could not walk fast enough to the local grocery store, H-E-B. Our house was within walking distance, and when the kids were at school, I would go and self-medicate to try and fill the gaping hole inside me. I got a cart and filled it with king-size candy bars of every kind—Snickers, Twix, and Hershey's were my favorites. I anxiously ripped open the Twix bar, devouring it as I casually dropped in a bag of Swedish Fish.

I scanned the aisles looking for my edible pain relievers. A chocolate cake, bag of Cheetos, corn chips, and a jar of Tostito's cheese dip were on the menu that day. I opened the bag of Cheetos and began shoving them in faster than I could chew. The hole was so deep inside that it was hard to fill up, but it didn't stop me from trying.

The donuts were calling my name. As I licked Cheetos dust off each finger, I scanned the donut section. I grabbed a glazed donut from the bakery case and immediately took a bite. Yep, yummy. I put the half-eaten donut in a pastry box. A chocolate-covered donut with sprinkles could not be missed. I grabbed it and ate the whole thing standing right there. The sugar rush was awesome. I took ten other donuts and bit into each one of them as I placed them in the box. I parked at a closed checkout aisle, took my food out, and set it on the ground. I was not hungry in a traditional sense, but starving in a "I can't get the food inside me fast enough" sort of way. If you watched me, you would have thought I had not eaten or seen food in months. But my figure suggested something else.

I sat on the ground next to the magazine rack. I pulled out several magazines and put the pile next to me with my food within reach. A few H-E-B workers walked past me, recognizing me from my frequent visits. Picking up the top magazine in my stack, I flopped it open on my lap, opened the donut box, and proceeded to eat every last one of them. Mmmmm, so good. The headline on the magazine stated that Carney Wilson had lost 150 lbs. after getting gastric bypass surgery and had gotten her excess skin removed. I grabbed the chips and cheese and flipped the page to continue reading her success story. Was this my answer?

I wanted to get the surgery after reading her story, but I had no way to pay for it. I brainstormed how I could make this happen as I flipped through the pages. I cracked the cheese dip jar open and dipped my chips, crunching through half the bag before finishing magazine two. Some cheese sauce spilled on my T-shirt. It was not as effortless as I made it look to eat on the hard store floors. I scraped the yellow sauce off my shirt with a chip but it stained the collar. I closed the lid to the jar of cheese and put the plastic top back on the eaten cake. I stood up, brushing some chocolate cake crumbs off me and pushed my cart to an open cashier. I placed the empty candy bar wrappers one by one on the conveyer belt. The man scanned them, looking up at me with a raised eyebrow. He opened the donut box and saw nothing but glaze stains inside.

"There were twelve," I informed him.

He closed the box and typed in the amount. He then proceeded to bag the candy bar wrappers, the empty jar of cheese, and the donut box. "Your total will be $23.48."

I dug my hand into my smelly, stained shirt and reached inside my bra for the credit card. He looked at the card and paused. He then grabbed a plastic bag from his rack, placed his hand in the bag like a makeshift glove, and used it to reach for the card.

"Would you like your receipt?" he asked, even though there was nothing left to return.

I shoved the credit card back in my bra. "No, thanks."

I was fat, getting fatter each day. I gained weight proportionally, which isn't as useful as it sounds when you're getting massive, because the fat becomes so contagious that suddenly you are fat everywhere. My eyes were the first things to disappear, and it became hard to distinguish what was a leg and what was an arm. I even went to the doctor when a large lump appeared on the back of my neck. I thought I had a cancerous growth, but without any testing the doctor assured me it was just fat.

I needed help controlling my overeating. I couldn't do it alone; I rushed home so I could start my research on gastric bypass surgery. I was a woman on a mission. I needed a job that would give me great health insurance because the insurance we currently had wouldn't cover gastric bypass surgery. I got a part-time job at a hospital as a phlebotomist that provided it. Once again, my career as a phlebotomist was paying dividends when it came to health insurance coverage.

One big roadblock was that to be a candidate for the surgery, patients had to have a body mass index (BMI) of 40, and I was at a 37. I made an appointment with a gastric bypass surgeon that week and needed to fix the problem quickly. I knew that I could not eat my way to a BMI of 40 in a week, but I tried. A surefire tactic I used was purchasing twelve ankle weights at Wal-Mart. I had my kids hold the weights while I duct-taped five ankle weights to each leg. I dropped some weights in my coat pockets for safe measure. I waddled into the doctor's office struggling to walk with all the added weight.

"Remove your coat and step on the scale," the nurse instructed.

With my heart pounding, I gently lay my ten-pound coat on the chair and stepped on the scale. The struggle of moving with the weights and my nerves were making me sweat and gasp for air. I needed this. This was my last hope to lose weight. I had tried everything! The number flickered on the scale. The nurse wrote down "248" on her clipboard. I relaxed and stepped off the scale. I qualified!

The week before the surgery I was weighed again, but this time I didn't have my weights with me. The number "238" flashed before my eyes. "Wow, you've lost some weight before the surgery!" the nurse congratulated me.

I lay in the pre-op hospital bed in my gown, the IV dripping in my arm, waiting to be taken to surgery. I felt nervous, but a sense of relief at the same time. My stomach was going to be so tiny there would be no way to shove in the type of food I had been downing for all these years. I thought of my kids coming home from school and seeing the Valentine's Day bags full of gifts I had left for them. I had to get well for them. I was getting dangerously overweight and at risk for diabetes.

The staff worker wheeled me into the operating room. It was ice cold. This was it and all my excitement turned into nerves. But, just maybe this was the answer, it had helped Carnie Wilson.

After my surgery we moved to Baton Rouge, Louisiana, for Mitch to become CEO of a hospital, part of the Ochsner health system. The recovery was slow and hard. I had an intense sensitivity to sugar. I tried to eat three Skittles but instantly threw up. My diet was restrictive but the surgery did work, I lost over a hundred pounds in a year, and with time my diet did normalize.

The darkness remained, but addressing my weight had removed a pain point. I saw many people eat through their gastric bypass surgery and gain all the weight back, but I didn't. Why did it work for me? Was it because I knew this was my final option? Was it because I never drank soda? There are so many unanswered questions in the world, and this is one of them. But for whatever reason, this was a miracle I was not going to question.

Several years after I had the gastric bypass surgery, my niece had her wedding in Sugar Land, Texas. We had lived in Texas when I was my fattest. At the wedding reception, I saw one of my old friends. I hugged her and asked how she was doing, but she looked at me, confused and asked who I was. I couldn't believe she didn't recognize me. We had been close friends for four years. I told her it was me, Sonja, and she instantly slapped her hand against her chest in shock. "When Mitch put his arm around you, I thought he divorced you and had gotten remarried," she told me. I didn't really know what to say to that, but I looked around the reception hall hoping that wasn't what everyone else thought. I felt the sudden need to wear a name tag proclaiming that "believe it or not, Mitch stayed married to fat Sonja!"

# CHAPTER 19

# Psych Ward

*Day Seven*

S onja, there's an urgent meeting you need to attend," a nurse said.

He walked me to a room I had not been to before. "Go in," he commanded. I opened the door and saw Mitch, seated next to my mother.

Jane had them pinned with her hard gaze, which then shifted in my direction. "Sit down, Sonja," she said.

Silently, I positioned myself next to Mitch and moved my hand to the arm of the chair, anxiously looking for his hand. It was my only source of comfort in such situations. But what kind of situation was this, exactly?

"Sonja is mentally ill, she's bipolar." Jane wasted no time letting Mitch and my mom know. She spoke as if I wasn't in the room and the words dropped like bombshells around us.

"What the hell do you mean I'm bipolar?" I inserted myself into the conversation. "You, Jane, have known me for six days. Have we even had a proper conversation, a real heart-to-heart?" I paused after posing the question, knowing she would not answer it. "No, we haven't." I gritted my teeth.

"Sonja!" my mom tried interrupting me, but I couldn't be stopped.

"How irresponsible of you, labeling me mentally ill. Are you even a doctor? Are you qualified to make that diagnosis?" I turned to Mitch. "You don't think I'm mentally ill, do you?" He looked just as scared and confused as I felt. "I don't know," he said. I could tell he was trying to avoid an argument.

"Your doctor diagnosed you as bipolar, Sonja," Jane answered. "You are mentally ill." She enjoyed saying it a little too much.

"Where's my doctor? Why is he not telling me my diagnosis? A real classy place you've got here. Real professional, Jane."

"It's a lifelong illness, you have to accept it." She stiffened.

"What if I don't? You think you're going to hand me a life sentence without a peep from me? Not a chance in hell!" I stood up and screamed.

"This family meeting is over!" Jane stood up. "You're not leaving here until you accept it. Do you hear me? You're not leaving this hospital until you admit you're bipolar!" She opened the door. "Nurses, come get Sonja."

I grabbed onto Mitch's arm. "Mitch, you've got to help me! Don't let her get away with this!" Two nurses grabbed my wrists and pulled me off him. "Mitch, this place is terrible! Stop them!" I cried out as they yanked me through the door. They dragged me into a holding room and locked the door behind them. I pounded my fists against the door. "Mitch! I'm in here!"

I leaned against the wall, wondering what they were telling Mitch and my mom about me. Was Mitch asking them to let me out or agreeing that I should stay longer? But hours passed and no one came to let me out. I was terrified of having the same illness as my grandfather, father, aunt, and some cousins as their horrible experiences with the illness filled my mind: jail, bizarre visions, bankruptcy, violence, and attempted suicide. I had personally known five people with mental illness who had committed suicide. I knew it was an illness that showed no mercy. If there were a definition of hell, I would say mental illness was it.

That night I was let out and brought to Dr. Barry. My bones felt hollowed, my body like a husk devoid of anything meaningful inside. I sat quietly, trying to figure out how I could put myself back together into something resembling a successful wife and mother.

"Sonja, you have to understand you are bipolar," Dr. Barry repeated a second time.

I was in a far, far away place and my doctor was beckoning me into the present moment.

"Are you listening to me?" He tried again. "Bipolar disorder is a genetic illness and it runs in your family. I have a folder here of your family history that lists other close family members suffering from the illness. How can you not see it is entirely plausible that you have it too?"

I finally looked at him. "I can't be bipolar."

"Well, you are. You've had manic and depressive episodes, reduced need for sleep, and lost touch with reality. Sonja, you have been extremely suicidal." He sighed. "There have been many times I was unsure of what diagnosis to give my patients, but with you, I'm one hundred percent certain. You. Are. Bipolar."

His confidence in my diagnosis absorbed any fight I had left in me to deny it. I already knew I had been living in hell, but I believed there was a way out someway or somehow. He just put a name to it—bipolar—which slammed the doors on any possibility that I could live a normal life. He stole that from me. I felt he was asking me to live an impossible life. It was a dagger to my heart that pierced with such precision, and I knew he was speaking a truth I had to face if I wanted to keep my family. I closed my eyes and mustered every ounce of courage, in every corner of my being, to accept this new reality that I would battle the rest of my life. It was not an illness that was curable, that was a fact I knew all too well.

"You're right, it's a family illness, and I guess I got nailed with it."

"Sonja, what illness do you have?" he pressed.

I knew what he wanted. I felt bile rising in my throat, leaving a slow, burning sensation in its path. My hands gripped each side of the chair until my knuckles turned white. My teeth clamped down on my lower lip, holding the words from being uttered to the point my lips started to bleed. An internal battle was being fought. Thoughts of my husband and children began pouring through my heart, and it was no contest. I knew who would win. Them. I would always choose them.

"I am bipolar."

# CHAPTER 20

# Psych Ward

*Day Eight, Final Day*

Everyone was eating breakfast, but I kept pacing in front of the big double doors. I couldn't eat; I was too excited to go home. Mitch would be coming through those cage-like doors any minute to take me home to our children. The minutes passed like sand in syrup, but when I heard the buzzer, I knew it was Mitch. The doors opened, and he stood between them holding cream roses. He looked excited and nervous, and with the flowers, he looked like he did on our first date. I ran into his arms, almost knocking him over.

"Ready to go home?" he whispered in my ear. The word "home" hit me, and I hugged him harder.

"Yes, please!"

He handed me the cream roses, which were my favorite. "Thank you, Mitch."

"I've missed you." His lips brushed mine, and I pressed into him, pushing our lips together. He gripped the small of my back, and I could feel his heart beating under my palm. We pulled away just a few inches, and our eyes met at the bridge of our noses, any distance was too far after how long we had been apart.

He took my hand. "Let's go." I loved this man. We were connected in a thousand ways that I never wanted to break. It would be
my life's goal to keep him. He was imperfect in a million ways. Mitch
could be irritable and impatient, but he was the person I needed him
to be when it mattered most. I felt he was a gift from my otherwise
silent God.

We walked outside to our car, and every tree and branch didn't
go unnoticed. Stepping outside, even in a parking lot, felt like such a
luxury. It was a freedom I would never take lightly again.

My mom, Allyson, and my three children were all waiting for me
when I walked into the house. I opened my arms wide, and my kids
ran into them. I gathered them as close as I could.

Mitch put his arms around the group hug. "It's good to have you
back."

Despite my discomfort with my diagnosis, Mitch was glad doctors had at least located the problem. Our plan was to have me take
the medication diligently and do therapy. For now, we could only
hope that would be enough.

# CHAPTER 21

# Home at Last

**M**itch's alarm went off, and the walls of our bedroom hit me with such familiarity it felt foreign. As Mitch threw off the white comforter and got in the shower, a rush of cold air slipped between the sheets as he left. These were the moments I longed for in the hospital, the ones I replayed in my mind, the ones I never thought I would miss until I did.

I swung my legs out from the covers, and the lazy Sunday sun lay across the carpet to warm my toes. I walked into our closet to find something to wear to church, and the walk-in closet instantly swallowed me.

Even though my wardrobe had only ever consisted of four colors (black, gray, white, and cream), I still had a lot to choose from. What I lacked in variety I made up for in quantity. I slipped a black silk dress off its hanger and stepped into it. I walked over to my dresser, which I had repurposed as a jewelry box. My collection was equal to that of a jewelry store. I ran my fingers across my armor. Jewelry was my obsession. How many gold bracelets would it take to get me through church today? I started piling them on each wrist and instantly felt better. I looked in the mirror, not connecting to the person who stood before me.

"Well. That's . . . a lot of bracelets," Mitch said with some concern. "But stunning as always." He kissed my cheek with a smile. Mitch was not flashy; despite being the CEO of the hospital, he drove a thirteen-year-old Honda Civic with a dent in the front.

Our little crew walked into church that morning and huddled onto a bench, acting like nothing dramatic had happened. I was pleased that Mitch and I could come to church and continue the appearance of being a normal family for our kids. We had remained stable during our consistently inconsistent lives.

Allyson sat on the other side of me, and my mom sat between the kids. The prelude music faded out, and the bishop went up to start the sacrament meeting. I sat in our pew with my hands resting on my lap. I couldn't believe I had been to a psych ward and back with no friends—in fact, nobody in the whole congregation, except my family members on this very bench—knowing about it. I was determined to keep this part of me so deeply hidden that it would feel like a dirty secret.

The next morning Mitch went off to work, and the kids were busy with their tutors, so my mom, Allyson, and I had most of the afternoon to ourselves. I drove us to the nearest mall to start our search for beautiful things.

"Let's stop in Ann Taylor," I said, halting before we passed the doors. There was nothing elegant about the way I shopped. My fingers didn't skim the racks of freshly sewn fabrics, and my feet most definitely didn't waltz through the aisles. When I walked into a store, I seemed like someone shopping for a uniform. So, as a creature of habit, that day in Ann Taylor was no different.

"Sonja, what about this?" My mom held up a purple-and-yellow floral shirt.

"No," I flatly responded.

"You would look gorgeous in it," my mom insisted.

"You know I just can't. I would put that on and want to throw up."

My mother tried again. "It'd be so pretty on you though."

"She doesn't wear color, Mom," Allyson said to her reflection as she held a yellow dress up to her shoulders.

"Oh, look, they have one in black and white!" My mom held up a striped version of the same dress.

"Or patterns." Allyson looked over her shoulder at our mom.

"But you love art. A lot of art has colors and patterns," my mom said.

"I'm fine with colors and patterns out there." I moved my arms in a circle, indicating the outside world. "I have enough chaos in my head, I don't need any more on me."

"Sonja, you can't wear black forever. You look like you're in mourning."

"It comforts me. The colors I wear are the only ones I can emotionally handle. Plus"—I looked at her with a smile—"white, black, and cream always match, so I rarely have to make fashion choices when I wake up." I had a hard enough time making small decisions like which bag of chips to buy or how many burritos to get from Taco Bell. I didn't need more choices waiting for me every day.

My mom held up a silk turquoise blouse with a matching skirt. "Could you do this? It's monochromatic."

I reached out and hesitantly touched the blouse. It really was beautiful. "I could try." I took the blouse and skirt from her and laid them on the cashier counter along with my black skirts.

"Dang, how many skirts are you getting?" Allyson laughed.

I tilted the stack up to my face and roughly counted. "Fifteen?"

"Did you see we have this skirt in other colors than black?" the cashier eagerly asked.

"Yeah, I just want the black." The cashier ripped the receipt off and handed me the ribbon handles to the bag.

Allyson put her arm around me. "You know I love you and your mourning clothes."

"And I love you in all your colorful ones." I smiled back.

CHAPTER 22

# The Routine

M itch dropped Allyson and my mom off at the airport. The house felt emptier without them, but I was ready to get back into my routine.

Every morning we stepped out of the car and walked into the humid Louisiana greenery onto the cracked tennis courts. The boys set their red water jugs down and jogged out to the middle of the court for warm-ups. I started my daily routine of lathering on inches of sunscreen and putting on my big hat for safe measure. We were always a half an hour early to practice serving to targets. Alex and Lincoln wanted to be professional tennis players; I took their dream seriously. I researched how many hours kids needed to practice to go pro and built a homeschooling schedule around those hours. They had a private tennis coach and practiced five to six hours a day, six days a week.

Once their tennis coach, Vincent, arrived, I picked up hundreds of tennis balls while the boys hit. Normally he would have the kids pick up balls after a tennis drill, but I quickly learned that if they were spending twenty percent of their time picking up tennis balls, they were wasting a lot of practice time. Rachael sat in one of the wobbly white plastic chairs and did homework under the shade of the only tree that leaned over into the court.

Aside from Vincent's coaching, the only sounds were the pop of tennis balls hitting thick racket strings or a tennis grunt when the boys hit the ball with all their might. Yellow fuzz flew over my head and rattled against the metal fence before falling into a bounce on the green concrete. I tried dodging as many as I could, but it was impossible to leave a practice without a few hits in the back, arm, or leg.

Hard work, dedication, excellence, and overcoming failure were important to our family values. Mitch had grown up working on his grandpa's farm in the summer to learn the value of hard work, and tennis was our kids' version of a farm. He saw the hard work as its own end, whether or not our sons ever became professional tennis players. But, doing all this for the sake of learning hard work was a concept I just couldn't wrap my head around. The investment we had made in tennis was substantial. We were spending over $30,000 a year in tennis lessons, shoes, rackets, and tournaments.

While Mitch was supportive, he did struggle at times, given the stress it caused in our finances. I appreciated that the boys were learning the value of hard work, but I needed a bigger payoff in exchange for the toll tennis was taking on me both personally and financially. I had told Mitch and Vincent many times that all this effort was only worth it if the boys went pro. It was all very black and white in my mind: either they become pro tennis players or stop lessons. I couldn't see a middle path where the boys did tennis for fun, made friends, and learned sportsmanship.

This mind-set put an enormous amount of pressure on myself and the boys. Each loss on the court was emotionally catastrophic for me, and each win was redemptive and addictive. With bipolar disorder, it had to be all or nothing, win or lose, a dichotomy that gave me some indescribably beautiful highs as well as devastating lows.

The problematic part of mania is that it can literally give you superhuman strength to work and achieve the impossible, but even with glorious mania, some things are out of your control and can set you up for disastrous defeats. Kids get injuries, games get rained out, and at times coaches give lousy advice. Mania could not solve everything, but its emotional force still ran through me like a freight train.

"Read your books," I told my kids as we got in the car. I always had them read while I drove. I was a stickler about not wasting time. One of our tutors called me a slave driver behind my back because I came off so intense.

As soon as we got home, the kids piled bottles of dish soap in their hands and ran outside under the carport for their thirty-minute break. They loved to fill my storage bins with water and soap to make their own tiny swimming pools. While the kids played, I prepared lunch and picked up my romance book. My mind moved at such an amazing speed at times that I could complete two or three books in a day. I kept three fifty-gallon storage bins to house all the romance books I had read in just a few years, as there was no place for them on the bookshelf. I put my book down and looked out the back-door window. Alex had his shirt off and sat in an old storage bin, chin high in bubbles. I opened the screen door. Alex turned to look at me through a pair of fogged-up goggles.

"Hey, Mom!" Water dumped over the rim of the gray bin when he shifted. I took a step back from the puddle and looked at all the empty Dawn bottles on the wet driveway covered in suds and smiled.

"Mom, look at mine!" Lincoln said as he finished squeezing the last bit of dish soap into his bucket. Rachael sprayed the hose into Lincoln's bucket, turning all his blue soap into foam.

I couldn't help but laugh as he strapped on a pair of goggles and dove in, struggling to get more than half of his face under water. He came up for air and wiped off the bubbles around his mouth.

"You can play for five more minutes. Your reading tutors will be here soon." I set a pile of towels on a patch of dry cement.

I went inside and pulled the surprisingly heavy Stouffer's lasagna out of the oven and set out plates. We lived on fast food and freezer meals. The kids came running in and scarfed down their food as Amy's little red car pulled in the driveway.

"Hi, Sonja!" Amy greeted me as she sidestepped around a puddle.

Natalie looked back at the bubble eruption and water-filled bins. "Well, that looks like fun!"

"Oh, I'm sure the kids will tell you all about it."

Usually I helped the tutors with the kids' reading, but I liked to deep clean after I had company, even if they weren't messy, so I started my ritual instead. I sprayed each bookshelf with lemon-scented wood polish and wiped it down with a cloth. The dust from the spray looked like heavy mist in the sunlight. As I reached for my cloth, an unexpected surge of panic grabbed me by the throat. I instantly dropped the dusting cloth and wrapped my hand around my neck. I struggled to breathe and my heart pounded so fast it rattled my insides. No matter how deeply I breathed, I could not get the air in fast enough. A heart attack? That had to be it. My ears started ringing as I sat on the carpet, struggling to breathe. I ran to my phone and dialed Mitch's number.

"Mitch, I can't breathe!" I tried not to cry, knowing that would only rob me of air.

"Seriously? Should I come get you? You need to get to the hospital," Mitch said.

"I'll have one of the tutors take me."

I stumbled to the playroom and gripped the doorway. "Can one of you take me to Mitch's office?" I whispered to the tutors as calmly as possible.

"Are you okay?" Amy asked, getting a better look at me.

"I think . . . I think I'm having a heart attack."

That got her attention. She dropped me off at the emergency room, where Mitch was waiting for me. He took me by the hand, and when we approached the front desk, the receptionist did a double take. It's not every day the CEO of the hospital comes to the emergency room for anything other than business. The receptionist picked up a phone to make a call, and within minutes we were in a room with several nurses.

"Sonja, you need to take deep breaths. You're hyperventilating," one nurse coached me while other nurses put warm blankets over me. The doctor opened the door and came to my bedside.

"I'm Dr. Griffin, and I'll be taking care of you today."

"Deep breaths, Mrs. Wasden," the nurse reminded me.

"I want to have your vitals checked before we do anything. Do you think you can help us do that?" Dr. Griffin gently asked.

I nodded and tried breathing slower, but my whole body was shaking. "Something's not right," I gasped.

"You're going to be okay." Mitch gripped my hand. But all I could feel was the burning in my chest and lack of air going to my head. If I was having a heart attack, I felt like I should be dead already.

Dr. Griffin came back in the room. "I want you to know your vitals and the ECG came back normal. Sonja, you're going to be just fine."

I didn't believe him. My body was in distress, and I needed medicine, surgery, something more than a pat on the back to get better.

"However, you are having an acute panic attack," he continued. "I'm going to have the nurses start an IV of Ativan to calm you down."

"Is it wrong that now I'm wishing it was a heart attack?" I whispered to Mitch. I'd had tons of panic attacks before, but this was different. It felt more physically distressing than any panic attack I'd had in the past. My body was literally shutting down.

"You'll need to go see your psychiatrist and set up a plan to deal with these attacks for the future."

The IV got started and whatever they had running through my veins took the pain away. My breathing regulated, and I could feel the oxygen satisfying my lungs. I drank my apple juice and snuggled into the warm blankets while we waited for the IV to finish. Once I was completely calmed down and full of drugs, Mitch and I left the hospital.

"Who's watching the kids?" I looked at the sky, realizing it was night.

"Don't worry, I called them and said we'd be home a little late. Rachael's got it covered." Mitch held my hand. "How are you feeling?"

"Better, but honestly, I don't want to make another plan with my psychiatrist and get more meds. I want to medicate myself."

"And how would you medicate yourself?" Mitch asked seriously, getting into the car.

I buckled myself in and thought about it. "Chocolate," I finally answered.

"What?" Mitch couldn't help but laugh.

"I would medicate myself with chocolate."

Mitch turned out of the parking garage and looked at me. "And you think that could help your anxiety?"

I looked back at him and shrugged. "Yeah?"

Mitch got quiet and turned on the radio. I looked out the passenger window at all the navy clouds and taillights reflecting in the rain on the street. I couldn't stop thinking about the panic attack I had just come out of; it felt like a near-death experience. That night I felt a lot like the puddles we were splashing through—cold and unsure if I would be there the next day. The car was suddenly parked and I did a double take before getting out.

"Why are we at Target?" I scoffed at the glowing red letters. Of all nights to stop and run an errand, tonight was clearly not the one.

"Well, Dr. Wasden, I think it's time you try your new prescription." He winked.

I sat staring at him and then bit my lip. That bright red sign didn't seem as obnoxious now. "How much chocolate can I buy?" I cut Mitch off before he could laugh. "That was a very serious question."

"As much as it takes. In your professional opinion, that is."

We stood in front of all my very closest friends—Godiva, Ghirardelli, Lindt—and all things dark chocolate. I filled our cart with every version those brands offered. As any doctor will tell you, there are hundreds of medications to try, and I was going to try them all.

"Do you think we got enough?" Mitch asked, placing the dark chocolate bags on the conveyer belt.

"I think we got every chocolate pill they offer." I pressed my lips against his. "Thank you," I whispered.

When we pulled into our driveway, I realized I had to find a place for all this chocolate. I walked into the kitchen and emptied a cupboard that famously became known as Mom's Chocolate Cupboard.

"You're home!" The kids ran to the door.

"Hey, stinkers!" Mitch set down his briefcase and hugged them. All at once the kids started telling him about tennis and Rachael's near miss in the face by Alex's tennis ball. He smiled and tried his best to follow their poor job at trading off storytelling.

"Well, you guys must be too tired for a Cowboy Johnny story after how crazy your day's been. You probably just want to go straight to bed," he said.

"No!" The kids panicked.

Mitch couldn't hide the smile at the corner of his mouth. He had created a story about a boy named Cowboy Johnny years ago and the idea stuck. Mitch's improvisational skills had gotten very good, and he could create a twenty-minute story within a few seconds.

"All right, maybe a short one!" Mitch changed out of his suit and led the kids upstairs. Even though they all had their own bedrooms, they preferred sleeping together in Lincoln's room. The boys crawled under the covers and Rachael curled up in her designated spot at the foot of the bed. It never looked terribly comfortable, but we let them.

"Do you all know what you want in the story?" Mitch asked the kids. It was a tradition that they each got to pick something that had to make an appearance in the story.

"A green cheetah!" Alex called out.

"A unicorn!" Rachael added.

"Lincoln, what do you want?" Alex asked.

"I want an egg."

"An egg?" Alex raised his eyebrows.

"All right, a cheetah, an egg, and a unicorn," Mitch said, sitting between the boys. "There once was a boy named Cowboy Johnny." He started with his opening line. Every night the kids listened intently for each of their animals to enter the story. I sat on the edge of the bed until the story was over.

"I want a trophy." Rachael yawned, looking at the boys' wall of tennis trophies.

"We can buy you one that says World's Best Daughter," Mitch said, as he tucked the boys in.

She turned to face him. "But I want to earn it."

"You have." Mitch kissed her forehead and turned out the light.

"Good night, kids. We love you," I said, slowly shutting the door. Mitch and I went downstairs to get ready for bed. I shook my pills out of their bottle into the palm of my hand. I looked at the blue-and-white pills and then swallowed them down with some tap water.

"You forgot one," Mitch said, holding out a small chocolate in his hand.

"I love you." I snatched the chocolate out of his hand and peeled off the wrapper.

# CHAPTER 23

# Let's Not Talk About It

As a recovering psych patient, I continued my visits with a psychiatrist. My new psychiatrist was Dr. Pope. He was much younger than Dr. Barry, and from my first impression of him, I could tell he would smile a lot more. He had brown hair, blue eyes, and a few freckles. His office had the requisite framed diplomas hung on his wall with the thin golden sticker proving their legitimacy, but my attention was pulled toward all the colorful artwork done by his children. Next to the watercolor paintings were pictures of his wife and kids at the beach. It brought positive energy into his small brown office.

"Sit down, sit down," Dr. Pope insisted in his friendly voice. He walked back to his desk and sat down. "So, Sonja, you recently got out of the hospital. How're you holding up?" He folded his hands and gave me a good look over.

"I'm not sure why, but I had a bad panic attack yesterday. I had to go to the ER," I said.

"I can get you a prescription that helps with severe panic attacks."

"Thanks." My eyes moved over to his pad of paper as he jotted down the medication.

"You also recently got diagnosed." Dr. Pope shifted in his seat, preparing himself for a long conversation.

"Yes, I'm bipolar, but we don't need to talk about it."

"Sonja"—he leaned forward with a small smile—"you're actually paying me to talk about it." He had me there.

"Well, all right, but only in this room." I hoped he would have some answers for me but doubted he would. "How do I know what's the disease and what is me?" I asked.

"That's the big question now, isn't it?" He folded his arms. "If you continue taking your medicine and do therapy, things will become more clear."

"Are you telling me, while I was unmedicated, most of my behavior and thoughts were because of the disease?"

"Yes, but now that you're medicated, you'll start feeling more yourself," Dr. Pope assured me.

How was I ever supposed to identify my real personality? I had not been medicated my whole life! And according to Dr. Pope, that probably meant I had not even met myself yet. So how was I supposed to recognize myself when and if I changed? The thought scared me. Who was I? Could I trust myself, my judgment, my choices? And how would I coexist with this all-encompassing disease?

Even though most of it comes down to good luck and genetics, we treasure so many things about our personality. It becomes hard not to consider the strangeness of those who are spared from mental illness simply because of biological chance. Somehow it feels unfair, even though no one is to blame.

"Let's talk about your childhood. How was that?" He leaned back in the black office chair.

"It was great. I had a perfect childhood."

"So, there is nothing in your childhood you have issues with?" he asked.

"Nope."

"Because it was perfect."

"Right."

"You really believe your childhood was perfect?"

"You keep asking the same question. My childhood and family are perfect. There's nothing more to investigate," I insisted.

"Bullshit."

I jerked my head back. "Excuse me?" I widened my eyes. He had my full attention.

"Bullshit," he said, calmer this time. "No one has a perfect family or childhood."

"Well, I did and still do. There are exceptions to everything."

"Your grandfather physically and verbally abused his ex-wives and children."

"He changed. Did you know three weeks before he died, he visited his oldest daughter and asked her to forgive him for all the times he hit her, and she asked him to forgive her for praying as a little girl that he would die? Then as my grandpa sat there in his wheelchair he told her, 'Don't forget! You and I are clean!' He wanted to repent. The grandpa I knew would line up his grandkids and ask for hugs and kisses in exchange for dollar bills."

"But Sonja—" Dr. Pope tried interrupting.

I continued. "Then my cousins and I would sit around and play poker with the money we got from him. He was a fun grandpa."

"What about the fact that he was married seven times, or that he held your grandmother at gunpoint, forcing her to remarry him a second time?" Dr. Pope challenged.

"Yes, but he *changed*," I reiterated. "My grandpa took us school shopping at Goodwill and bought us real wedding dresses for dress up. He even took us on his garbage runs. We would get in dumpsters and fish out all the good stuff stores had thrown away. Then you know what we would do with that stuff? We would take it to the poor. He did a lot of good."

"But he also threatened to kill his wife."

"Why do you keep bringing that up? What's your point?" I snapped.

"That mental illness has an ugly side that you seem set on blocking out. I'm not saying your grandpa was all bad. I know he changed for the good later in his life. But you're not acknowledging the things he did when he was sick."

"That's not true."

"Sonja, I'm not just talking about oddities."

I held my hand up. "Let me finish. When I was sixteen, he prophesied that I would die in a car wreck, and he'd take my body up a mountain and bring me back to life. Believe it or not, Doctor, even a woman straight out of a mental hospital knows an old man's belief that he can resurrect his granddaughter is bizarre."

"That's a start, but we've got a long way to go. You see things in black and white. You think things are perfect or horrible when most of the time it's probably somewhere in the middle."

I shrugged. "Maybe that's true."

# CHAPTER 24

# Damaged Goods

I would rather be ashes than dust!
I would rather that my spark should burn out
in a brilliant blaze than it should be stifled by dry-rot.
I would rather be a superb meteor, every atom
of me in magnificent glow, than a sleepy and permanent planet.
The function of man is to live, not to exist.
I shall not waste my days trying to prolong them.
I shall use my time.

—Jack London's "Credo"

Rachael held up the sheets of printed poems. "Why are we writing all this?" she asked from the back seat of the car.

"Because one day, you might need some encouragement and these poems could say things how you need to hear them." I handed her a notebook and pen.

"So, are we going to fill all the pages?" Alex asked, flipping through all the blank sheets of his notebook.

"Not today. Just copy down two that stand out to you."

I played the Disney *Tarzan* soundtrack while I drove to Wal-Mart, occasionally checking the kids in the rearview mirror to see if they were still writing. It was a Saturday, and Mitch had stayed home to work on his doctorate he was getting from George Washington University while working full-time. His time had been so limited that he completely cut out television and hobbies during the four years he was enrolled.

I pulled into Wal-Mart, and the kids grabbed a grocery cart. They followed behind me through the rows of cereal boxes and trail mix. I stared at all the options, unsure why I was even in that section of the store. I put two boxes of Raisin Bran in the cart and moved to the chip aisle.

"Let's get these!" Alex held up two bags of his favorite salt-and-vinegar chips and put them in the cart.

"What did we need to get?" I blanked.

"Tortilla chips are good," Alex suggested. I looked at the rows of corn chips and knew we needed them. I just didn't know which ones to get. So many choices; I felt overwhelmed. I put five bags in the cart and hovered over a sixth bag. Hint of Lime, On the Border, Yellow Corn, Blue Corn, Organic Black Bean, Thin and Crispy, Lightly Salted, Santitas.

"Which one?" I desperately asked, holding two bags up to my kids.

"Um, On the Border?" Rachael replied.

I looked at the two bags. "Why not Thin and Crispy?"

"I don't know, I've never tried that."

I put two bags of On the Border chips in the cart. "Should I get another bag or is this enough?"

"Mom, this is plenty! I'd put some back," Rachael said, reaching into the cart.

"No, leave it! I think we need more." I couldn't grasp what amount of chips would last us through the week. "How fast will you guys eat these?" I asked, putting another bag in the cart.

"Not fast enough," Rachael said under her breath.

"Just tell me a number. Do we need four bags or five?" I felt completely confused like I was stuck on a math problem so long that none of the numbers looked familiar.

"Two," Rachael said firmly. "We only need two bags of chips."

"Two? But I have seven!" The thought of removing bags felt more complicated than adding bags. "I'm going to put one more in." I reached for another bag.

"Mom, no." Rachael took the bag out of my hand.

"Seven isn't enough." Even in my confusion, I felt that had to be true.

"Okay, let's get three then," Rachael said softly.

"Just one more than two? No, we need more than that!" I panicked and dumped three more bags in the cart.

"You're right. Let's get another one, for safe measure." She looked at me like I was a child she did not want to set off. "I think ten bags is good." She pushed the cart out of the chip aisle before I could second-guess the number.

We strolled through the cheese aisle, and I stacked five blocks of cheese in the cart. Rachael looked back with a raised eyebrow but didn't say anything, afraid it would only escalate the situation to ten blocks of cheese. We checked out of Wal-Mart and headed to the bookstore.

Our car tires splashed through the rain in the Barnes & Noble parking lot, and the kids ran to the front doors. The aroma of coffee beans and vanilla seemed to be the ever-present welcome of the bookstore. The permanent scent never lingered between the covers of any book though. Each page still smelled of raw paper and ink, which was one of Barnes & Noble's best qualities.

"Mom, let's start in the kids' section!" Lincoln tugged my hand behind him as we walked to the room in the back with the fake trees and the green frog in overalls always climbing step two of the ladder. He ran off to the stuffed animals, and I waited for him at one of the benches by the wooden train set.

A little blond girl set Thomas the Tank Engine's black wheels in the grooves of the wooden track after her brother had crashed it off the table. She clipped magnetic train cars together, but only got to car four before her little brother swiped Thomas off the track again. "Come over here." A short, blond woman sweetly picked them up. "Let's read a book." The two kids sat in their mom's lap in front of the book, which was spread wide.

As I looked at the seemingly perfect family, I thought back to Dr. Barry's comment about parenting. I wondered if that young mom who was spending her afternoon in the children's section of Barnes &

Noble, watching them play with trains, also scarred her kids. I wondered if all parents really did unintentionally harm their kids. What was a normal threshold of harm? Or at least the average damage done to a child? I clenched my fist under my chin and stared with what I'm sure was a little too much intensity at the two toddlers in her lap. They looked safe and happy, and as much as I wanted to believe I harmed my kids no differently than the cute mom in blue jeans, I knew I had undoubtedly harmed my kids in ways she never had. I slammed the brakes at these thoughts that would destroy me and decided to see myself in that young mom. I, like her, was also at Barnes & Noble with my kids whom I fiercely loved. At least for today, that was enough.

"Mom, can I get this one?" Lincoln held up a fluffy puppy dog toy with a brown patch over one eye.

"Sure, but can you still find a book? We're going to take turns reading to Dad when we get home."

Lincoln's eyes lit up. "This dog comes with a book!" He ran to where he found the dog and brought back a chapter book with a cartoon version of the dog on the cover.

I thumbed through the pages. "Sure, that'll work." I closed the book and tucked it under my arm. My eyelids started to feel heavy, and my arms felt weak. A family bustled around me to the books on sale, and I leaned against a bookshelf for some stability. These horrible meds were wreaking havoc on my life. Everyone around me seemed to be enjoying themselves; I envied that. I was in the same place they were, looking through the same books, yet I felt like the only one unable to take it all in. I wanted to be them. I wanted normal. My eyelids closed without my permission, and I knew I needed to get home before I fell asleep.

I dumped my stack of books on the customer-service desk and turned away to scream to the kids that we were leaving. I pushed my way past people on my way out. Hobbling through the parking lot, I held my eyes open with my fingers.

"Mom, what's wrong?" Alex asked, squinting at me.

"My medicine's making me fall asleep."

I sped home driving with one hand on the wheel and one hand holding an eye open so I would not get in a wreck. I barely made it back safely with the kids. I ran through the front door and yelled for Mitch.

"What is it, Sony?" Mitch came running.

"I'm falling asleep! Help me stay awake!"

Mitch took my hand and led me to the bedroom. "The meds again? Come over here. I'll lie down with you."

"No! I don't want to go to sleep. Do you understand me? It's not fair!" I started sobbing. "Mitch, I can't do this. I can't live like this. What kind of life is this?" I hated it. I hated having no say when I went to sleep. I constantly had to leave stores, movies, friends, all because my medication knocked me out right as I was starting my day.

Mitch sat on the bed and held his hand out. "Come here, Sony, want me to brush your hair?" Usually having my hair brushed helped calm me down, but not this time.

I ignored him and paced across my bedroom floor, fighting to stay awake. I breathed in through my nose, and it stung the same way chlorine stung when it got up my nose. This lifelong illness affected my weekdays, weekends, and every moment in between. I could not get away from the symptoms of my bipolar disease, yet I wanted to treat it like a painful part-time job. I wanted a doctor to tell me when to clock in and when to clock out; I'd work hard and deal with all the bad customers that fill my head, but in return, I wanted days off. My doctor said this was a lifelong illness, but even lifelong careers got holidays. I had to prove to myself that lifelong did not have to be the same as a life sentence.

I slowly awakened. How did I get in my bed? Probably Mitch. I took a deep breath. Heavy blankets from all over the house were sprawled over me. In a sweaty blur, I tiredly flung my foot around until I managed to kick a few blankets off the bed. The side of my neck felt warm where something furry was caught under my chin. I picked it up and squinted at the little yellow-and-brown dog. It was Lincoln's toy from the bookstore. I took another deep breath. I had survived. I heard plastic bags being shuffled around and the kids laughing.

"Wow, this is a lot of chips! I guess we're having nachos for dinner . . . again." Mitch's voice echoed from downstairs. I walked into the kitchen.

"Good afternoon, feel better?" Mitch asked.

"How'd I get in bed?" I wanted to know.

"Dad carried you like a bride." Rachael clasped her hands together and fluttered her eyelashes.

"A dead bride." Alex laughed.

"No, Mom looked like Sleeping Beauty," Mitch corrected, ruffling up Alex's hair.

"We went back to Barnes & Noble and got the books," Lincoln said.

"The kids took good care of you while you were sleeping. They each picked out a blanket for you." Mitch patted my leg.

"I put my dog, Spot, in the blankets with you." Lincoln pointed to the dog.

I handed him the little stuffed animal. "Thanks, Lincoln."

"Tomorrow's your first day of the intensive outpatient program." Mitch nudged me with his elbow. "It's like your first day of school. Do you need any lunch money?" he joked.

"No." I shot him a glare.

Therapy in a group setting felt slightly more comfortable for the fact that the therapist would not be focused on me the whole time. I hoped it would be a classroom setting where the therapist mostly lectured and didn't require much participation.

# CHAPTER 25

# You Get Me

I walked into the Intensive Outpatient Program and saw all the chairs formed a circle. There were only two people in the small gray room: a blond woman and a young man with a stack of blank printer paper. It seemed the only reason he had brought the papers was to stack and reshuffle them obsessively.

"Will you stop that?" the blond woman exploded. "It's so annoying!"

"Sorry." He gathered up the papers, enjoying his first practical shuffle, and tucked them under his chair. Two minutes into the silence he started fidgeting in his chair until he reached down to get his papers and started shuffling again. It was obvious he could not help himself. I wondered how he went grocery shopping or watched TV with his rather large stack of papers.

More people came into the room and filled the empty seats. A man wearing the equivalent of a Halloween lumberjack costume came and sat next to me. He kept his head down, and his eyes didn't shift once from his steel-toed boots.

"Okay, I believe everyone is here." A woman in a light blue suit shut the white door behind her and walked across the carpet to find a seat. "Let's get started." She crossed her legs and leaned over her knees, appearing friendlier than my first impression led me to believe. "Say your name and something you want to improve." She pointed to Mr. Lumberjack next to me. "Would you mind starting?"

"I'm Kent." His beard stayed tucked under the collar of his flannel shirt. "I like to set stumps on fire." He tapped the heels of his boots together. "So, I would like to find more tree stumps to burn, 'cause I'm running out."

The blond woman went next. "I'm Sherri." She smiled and waved to the class. "I have anxiety and depression. I want to cut my Xanax meds down to three times a day instead of six so I can hold down a job." When she finished, she looked to her left, waiting for the paper shuffler to go next. He looked up nervously and fumbled through his pages.

"Brad, it's your turn," the therapist prompted. His eyes widened as he looked around the room and shook his head no. "Okay, maybe next time." The therapist smiled.

It was my turn. "Hi, I'm Sonja, and I'm bipolar. I haven't showered in ten days, so my goal is to shower twice a week."

Sherri jumped up to her feet. "Oh my gosh, me too!" She slapped her hands on her thighs, laughing. "I'm not the only one!"

"No. You're definitely not. Showering's really hard for me. My husband can't understand it," I said.

Sherri sat back down. "You get me!" She pointed at me across the room.

"Okay, next." The therapist moved on, getting us back on track.

"I'm Karen. I suffer from depression. I just want to feel joy again. That is my goal."

"Karen, you'll get through this darkness and won't always feel this way. It will go away," the therapist reassured her.

My head perked up. The words "it will go away" had my heart pounding with hope.

"It will?" I asked.

The therapist looked at me. "Now, let's not compare ourselves with each other. Everyone here has different struggles. Sonja, there are environmental and biological illnesses. I know from Karen's diagnosis hers is environmental so hers will pass, but yours is biological, so it won't."

"Sounds interesting." I pulled my car up to Carla's house. She was my polygamist friend. Carla had more brothers and sisters than I could ever remember, twenty-six or something. I do not even know how many women her dad was married to. She had a sister wife once, but the woman ran off. She and her husband never knew what happened to her.

Carla and I met at church and instantly hit it off. Even though she was not part of my church, she occasionally attended our services. We most certainly had different beliefs, but we respected and loved each other.

Carla opened the door with her huge smile and arms open wide. "Sonja! Come in, come in!" I smiled and hugged her back.

"Are my boys ready to be picked up?" I asked.

"They're in the backyard playing. Come sit. Are you hungry? Want a drink or anything?" Carla picked up her newborn baby as I sat on the couch.

"No, I'm fine, but thanks," I said.

"We're thinking about leaving for Mexico soon." She patted her baby on the back. "America's getting less safe by the day."

"Where will you stay in Mexico?" I asked.

She pulled a paper off the counter and handed it to me. It looked like a hand-drawn treasure map. She had drawn a very rough sketch of how to get there, and a little house sat at the X. I handed her back the paper, but she pushed her palm forward, rejecting it.

"Keep it. When America falls, you and your family can come stay with us."

It was a kind gesture, letting us have the directions to her small Independent Polygamist community in Mexico.

"Thanks." I tucked the paper into my pocket. "I'm going to miss you and your awesome homemade bread."

"You could come with us, you know."

"I know, you're so sweet, Carla. But our life is here in Baton Rouge. Mitch was just promoted to CEO of the hospital. His career is here. He just couldn't leave the hospital without notice."

"Just remember you are always welcome." She rocked her baby.

"I know." I smiled. The thought of dropping everything and going with her to Mexico seemed exciting and scary at the same time.

On my way home I thought about Carla. She was afraid America was going to fall and the only safe refuge was her community in Mexico. Living life in a state of fear was all too familiar. Even though hers and mine were different fears, it still played a big part in our daily existence. I felt afraid of my disease and sometimes of myself. Carla was afraid of America. We both lived in fear, and we both chose to run, only she was a lot more cheerful than I was. It was an odd mix: sweet, cheerful, fearful. But nevertheless, it was still fear.

CHAPTER 26

# Calm in the Storm

All of Louisiana was preparing for Hurricane Gustav to hit in two weeks, except for the Wasden family. Looking back, I cannot believe we didn't take the warnings more seriously, but we had never prepared for a hurricane. So, we found ourselves in a postapocalyptic Wal-Mart three days before the storm. Our cart rattled down the canned food section that didn't have a single can of food. Oh, wait, that's not true. There was a dented can of corn that had rolled under a shelf. I leaned down and put it in our cart.

"Do you have any more canned food in the back?" I asked one of the four Wal-Mart employees in the store.

"Nope, everything's been cleared out," an unhelpful employee in a green collared shirt replied.

The kids found it all very exciting. They had never seen a major grocery store empty before. We checked the cereal, trail mix, frozen dinners, and candy sections, each with the same underwhelming conclusion. Rachael thought this was the coolest place to play Survivor. Alex and Lincoln followed her down the aisles, pretending there was a high-risk war outside and they had to live in the store for the next month.

"Come on, little scavengers," I yelled behind me on my way to check out. The cashier scanned my four items. One dented can of corn, a mandarin orange fruit cup, a box of Grape-Nuts cereal (it was the only selection left), and a can of Easy Cheese. I was not too worried since Mitch had insisted we keep food storage for emergencies. We had things like oats, pancake mix, powdered eggs, and honey that could feed us for a few months and a barrel of water. I just was not a great cook, so I was hoping to get a bunch of canned food.

The day of the hurricane we began our schoolwork routine like any typical day. Since Mitch was the CEO of a hospital, he had to sleep at work and stay there throughout the storm and its aftermath. The hurricane would be hitting within hours. I looked outside our playroom windows, but nothing seemed out of the ordinary. It was the calm before the storm. I was talking to my mom on the phone when the storm started. Rain, wind, and twigs began bouncing off the windows. Then my phone went dead.

The kids and I sat huddled on the couch as we watched pieces of our roof fly by the windows. The lights flickered off and on again. We froze, and then went back to watching the wind rip leaves off trees. The house creaked, and branches from our huge oak tree snapped to the ground. It was hard to see what was going on outside through the sheets of rain. However, we did see a tree fall right into our neighbor's house, cutting it in half. Oddly, I was unafraid. It felt almost calming to me. "Power's out," Alex said, flicking the light switch up and down.

Even though the news discouraged being by windows, we went upstairs to the playroom and sat on the carpet playing Five Crowns in the dim light. It did not take long for the whole house to feel like a sauna. Louisiana was humid enough, but add a tropical storm and the air was a hundred percent warm mist.

"It's so hot." Rachael squirmed on the floor.

"Go change into some shorts," I said, sliding the cards into their purple cardboard box.

Once the storm had passed, we walked outside to see that several more trees had fallen into houses. Neighbors walked the streets, discussing the disaster and the mess we were surrounded by, but when

I looked around, I did not see what they saw. I felt like I was in a modern art museum. I saw original shapes and designs all around me. Hundred-year-old oak trees were torn up from the ground exposing a maze of roots. They created a beautiful design of flawlessly intertwined lines with dark green grass sticking out looking like brushstrokes against dark brown dirt playing as its background. Downed power lines looked like Jackson Pollock had dripped lines of paint across the streets. Branches, leaves, flowers, and roof shingles covered the ground, creating patterns that my hands itched to paint. But I no longer had paint, canvases, or brushes. I gave that all up long ago, so I painted and designed in my head, in secret.

In an odd way, seeing all my neighbors share an epic and common misfortune made me feel at ease like we were in something together when I had been feeling so alone and isolated.

When the sun set that day, the house was completely dark. I had not realized how much I relied on the lights until they were gone, but it did not bother me. Darkness I was familiar with and had dealt with. It just entered the real world, which I liked. We ate Chef Boyardee straight from the can in the dark, brushed our teeth in the dark, and walked to bed in the dark. The electricity did not come back on for another thirteen days. The kids and I saw Mitch only after the roads had been cleared of power lines and debris. He had to stay at the hospital and make sure the generators were working and the patients were still able to receive care. People were going crazy, but not me. We were all trapped in our houses, but unlike this temporary storm, the storm trapped inside my body was going nowhere. It was my unwavering companion. So, for this short while, I actually felt normal. For once, my outside world matched my inside world: complete chaos and darkness.

# CHAPTER 27

# Mrs. Johnson

I was constantly weighed down by the pressure to ensure my children had the best education. I spent hours teaching, studying, and writing with them. I always thought I could not do enough to educate them. So, we did homework every day of the week, including vacation. During the summer I always took an extra suitcase full of schoolwork. I even had all three of my kids enrolled in Baton Rouge Fine Art Academy—an incredible two-year art program—on top of everything. We changed up our school routine from only private tutors and myself (all with different degrees) to adding a half day at a school run by an elderly couple from New York who rented out a trailer where they taught K-12.

When we walked into the small trailer, we saw fifteen kids total. The school was one big room filled with tables and chairs. The elderly couple, Mr. and Mrs. Johnson, had hired two other people to teach alongside them: an elementary school teacher and a math teacher. Mrs. Johnson's specialty was English and Mr. Johnson—bless his heart—was so old and frail he mostly walked around the room with his cane until Mrs. Johnson demanded he sit back down. Unlike her husband, Mrs. Johnson was an energetic, four-foot-tall woman who led the loudest and proudest Bible hour I'd ever seen. Her political tangents were legendary and why she was so famously quoted in our house.

After school and tennis, I drove the kids home. When we passed the FOR SALE sign in our yard, I realized Mitch and I should take it down at this point. It had been three years, and our house had not sold. We had spent more than we had anticipated renovating the house. With the renovation, private tutors for three kids, and tennis lessons, we felt we needed to downsize. But the emotional toll of the house not selling was creating more problems in our marriage. The next week, after talking it over with Mitch, we took our house off the market. It felt nice driving home without the reminder that our home was only temporary.

I called my dad while tidying up the kids' playroom. As I waited for him to pick up the phone, I pulled a few small stuffed animals from the toy chest and added them to my personal collection. I carried stuffed animals around and slept with them when I felt under stress.

My dad answered after the third ring. "Sonja! It's so good to hear from you!" he yelled into the phone as he smacked his gum.

"How have you and Mom been?" I asked, trying to appear somewhat upbeat.

"Just great! But did your mom tell you about Brandon Curtis?"

"No, who's that?"

"Brandon Curtis was a football player who died doing donuts in the Springville High School parking lot with his friends. The car flipped."

"That's terrible, Dad. I'm sorry to hear that." Death constantly clung to my daily thoughts, yet so many people died who didn't want to.

My dad started a passionate rant. "Brandon donated seven major organs, which saved many people's lives! Sonja, organ donation is a divine cause. It's such a selfless gift of love." My dad was not just interested in organ donation; at times it could completely consume all of his thoughts, finances, and communication with friends and family.

"Wow!" I leaned the phone against my ear. "That's—"

"Imagine if everyone was an organ donor, how many lives we'd save!"

Organ donation was my dad's obsession, his trigger. He had started a foundation called The Gift of Life and began his dream of creating a memorial for those who had died and donated their organs. Working with Intermountain Donor Services, he raised money to help build a tall glass wall with donors' names engraved on it at Library Square in Salt Lake City but ended up paying for the memorial mostly himself. While it was an amazing memorial, I had mixed feelings about it because this cause was what brought my dad's mania out in full force. I heard the kids run up the stairs from playing outside.

"Mom! Can you help me heat up the oven for the pizza?" Lincoln asked from down the hall.

"Hey, Dad, I—"

"The state of Utah could save four thousand or more people!"

"Dad, I—"

"We're going to start campaigning tomorrow! T-shirts, wristbands, all in the name of Brandon Curtis!"

I knew my dad well enough to know when he was talking on autopilot. He could talk for hours without needing any sort of feedback to continue. I set the phone down and went to put the pizza in the oven. Then I ran back upstairs to the playroom, hoping my dad hadn't noticed I was not there. I picked up the phone off the bookshelf, put it to my ear, and he was still going as if someone had been on the line for the last thirty minutes.

"So, on August 28th it's going to be Brandon Curtis Make a Difference Day. We teamed up with the Utah Organ Donor Coalition and a group of his friends will be helping to organize the fund-raiser. We're going to have a Brandon Curtis Scholarship and try to break the Guinness Book of World Records with the most people signed up for organ donation in a day."

"That's a lot of work, Dad. I'm sure Brandon Curtis's parents appreciate it."

"Yeah, I've been going over to their house every day, counseling and emotionally supporting them." I wondered if he was smothering them, taking it too far. They were grieving for their son, and I hoped he also gave them the space they needed.

"It's a heavenly cause! Saving lives!" he shouted through the phone. Mitch tried calling me while my dad continued. "Suzanne's going to help me see this through, and we're going to have a celebration with food and a bouncy castle for the kids—"

"Dad, I have to go, Mitch is calling, I'll call you back later." I hung up and accepted Mitch's call.

"Hey Mitter, what's up?"

"I have some big news for you when I get home." I could hear him trying to keep his excitement level measured.

"What is it?" I asked, hoping for a little good news to balance out my day.

"I want to tell you in person. I'll be home in twenty minutes."

I hated suspense. I sat staring at the patterns in the wood table so long, I could have drawn them from memory. I heard Mitch's car pull in and ran to the carport.

"Sooooooo?" I impatiently opened his door for him.

He stepped out of the car and straightened his tie. "I got a call from a recruiter today. They want me to apply for a Chief Operating Officer position at Covenant Healthcare in Lubbock, Texas."

The word "Texas" had me jumping up and down inside. I loved living in Texas.

"Whoa," was all that fell out of my mouth. "Do you want to apply for it?" I asked, full of hope.

"Yeah, I think I do. It would be a great career opportunity. Also, that's where I graduated from high school, and you loved Texas when we lived in Sugar Land. Obviously, we'll pray about it, but what do you think?"

"Mitch, we could stay there for ten to twenty years. You could move up and become the CEO when the current CEO retires. We could finally settle somewhere."

It seemed too good to be true. Mitch grabbed my hand and continued talking about all the benefits of the job as we went into the house. "But who knows, I probably won't even get it. The recruiter said there are already more than twenty candidates."

The possibility of moving would consume us. We would start looking at houses in the area "for fun," and then our hearts would jump when we thought about the salary increase. We'd get nervous before interviews and get nervous after interviews. And when we weren't casually watching for Mitch's phone to ring, we were mentally preparing ourselves for the long road ahead because the entire process took up to six months.

I was mostly concerned that he would not get the job. As fate would have it, any job Mitch didn't get, he would always make it to the final two. We had done this process countless times before, so I had to be sure I was ready to ride this roller coaster with him once again.

Months passed, and Mitch made it past the third round of interviews. Now we were waiting for a phone call to see if he made it to the final two. I dropped the kids off at school and stopped at Wal-Mart on the way home to pick up more medication, the chocolate kind. My coat pocket started vibrating, and my hand fumbled in the pocket before pulling out the phone.

"My name is Nancy," a woman's voice said. False alarm. Letting out a nervous breath, I leaned my ear against my shoulder. "I know your house is off the market, but I have someone who wants to buy your home."

"What?" I yelled louder than intended. Scooting my cart down the candy aisle, I focused in on the details Nancy gave me. Our house was finally selling! I threw a few chocolate bags in the cart and tried to call Mitch. The phone rang once, and he picked up.

"I was just about to call you. I made it to the final two!"

"Mitch, you'll never believe it, a realtor just called and said someone wants to buy our house, and we didn't even have it for sale."

"Seriously?" Mitch's shock sounded just like mine a few moments earlier.

"Mitch, this job in Lubbock is meant to be! God is paving the way for us."

"The recruiter said they want us to fly out in two weeks for the on-site interview."

"Mitch, I'm so ready for this!"

When the plane landed, Lubbock was as hot and dry as the Texas I remembered, and I loved it. A realtor took me around to look at houses while Mitch interviewed all day. I found the perfect house. It was cream with dark wood, and I couldn't help but fall in love. I knew this would be our future home. It was gorgeous.

Dinner that night with the team felt natural, and the conversation flowed. Later, the recruiter called Mitch and told him to prepare himself for an offer. We flew back home on cloud nine. So, we went ahead and sold our house, moved everything into a storage unit, and moved into a two-bedroom apartment while we waited to hear back. Moving to Texas couldn't come soon enough.

# CHAPTER 28

# Role Reversal

Mental illness laced its way through my family tree like an unpredictable virus affecting everyone without warning. No one was left untouched. My dad had just unofficially adopted a Hispanic family he met in a parking lot. When he tried to throw a random party for them, he got so agitated and demanding at the party store the cashier got scared and called 911. The police came and removed him from the store. He was also becoming delusional. One night he was at the cemetery talking to his dead father who he claimed was instructing him how to solve the organ-donation crisis. Someone called the police and my dad was taken to the police station. My brother had to come get my dad and convince the police that he would take care of him.

Even though my dad was clearly sick, his psychiatrist refused to send him to the psych ward against his will. My dad could be so convincing and charming, duping even well-trained psychiatrists was not hard for him. Many of my brothers and sisters tried to hospitalize him with no success. His friends had even written his doctor multiple letters saying, "Please hospitalize him, this is not the David we know." But the doctor continued to believe my dad and would only admit him if a family member insisted he was at risk of hurting himself or others. At this point, I flew to Utah, determined to get my dad hospitalized. The irony of our role reversal was not lost on me.

Mitch pulled the car around to the airport passenger drop-off and handed me my bag. He pulled me in and kissed my forehead. "Call me when you land."

"I will," I said into his shoulder as we hugged. "Pray for me."

"You're very brave, Sonja," Mitch said, squeezing my hand.

"I don't feel brave," I said.

"You're one of the bravest people I know," he insisted. "Don't worry about us. I'll take care of the kids and hold down the fort." I kissed him goodbye.

My mom picked me up from the airport but was silent on the car ride home.

"So, where's Dad?" I asked, looking forward. I hoped the lack of eye contact would help her answer me openly.

"I don't know." She shifted in her seat and re-gripped the steering wheel.

"Is it true he got banned from Springville High School?" My siblings told me that my dad threw packs of gum on the football field for the players during the game and advised the coach what players to put in. The cops escorted him off school property after he started dancing on the field with the cheerleaders.

After a long pause, my mom could only say, "Well, there's no sense in talking about it."

We drove up the long, steep driveway to my childhood home. As much as I did not look forward to this visit, it did feel good to be home.

As my mom and I walked down the dark green–carpeted hallway, I glanced at all the famous art lining the walls and remembered my dad making fun of how clumsy I was. He would say, "Whenever Sonja walks down that hall, paintings just fall behind her."

My mom and I continued to walk to the front entrance that boasted white marble floors, gold leafing, a massive chandelier with sculpted horses coming out of the relief on the ceiling, and two staircases ascending on the right and the left. I wondered if my dad was in his usual spot upstairs in his room, on the phone, holding his yellow notepad.

My mom and I climbed the stairs. I opened the tall wooden doors to my parents' bedroom and peeked in, but he wasn't there.

"I moved him to the guesthouse," my mom informed me.

"That's sad," I commented.

"But necessary for the time being. You can put your bag in here and sleep with me."

We went to sleep that night with my mom locking the bedroom door. She turned the clock toward her as she got into bed. Being home, under that same blanket with my mother, tricked me into a sense of parental comfort that did not exist at the moment. We lay awake not talking, waiting for my dad to come home. He wandered the streets at night. I did not know what he was doing and my mom was not a talker. There were many layers to my mom and her life, which she mostly didn't share with me.

The lights outside flipped on, and we heard my dad come into the guesthouse. My mom looked at the time and scribbled down "3:30 A.M." on a piece of paper. I assumed the doctors asked her to keep track of his sleeping habits. I fell asleep that night with nerves in my stomach, knowing tomorrow was the day I was going to hospitalize my dad.

That morning I jumped out of bed to get to the guesthouse before he woke up and started his scattered day. His appointment was not until 3 P.M., so I planned on spending the earlier part of the day with him to make sure I got him there. When I came down the stairs, I found him sleeping on the couch with a newspaper over his belly. Phew, I hadn't missed him. I ate breakfast and texted Mitch while continually checking that my dad was still on the couch. After an hour, I heard the newspaper fold and my dad sit up. One suspender strap hung off his shoulder, and he had major bed head, which with his wispy gray comb-over was quite endearing. He stood up in his slippers and rubbed his eyes.

"Hi, Dad!" I walked over to the couch and hugged him. I tried to take in the warm hug he tiredly offered back. "I'm going to spend the day with you. Do you have anywhere you need to be?"

"You need to meet the family I adopted. But first, let's go grocery shopping." He put a pen in his shirt pocket and patted his pants for his wallet.

"It's on the counter." I handed him his stuffed brown wallet. "You adopted a family?"

"You'll love them." He shuffled his slippers across the floor and headed toward the car. I got into the passenger side and listened to him make several seemingly urgent phone calls about his organ donation.

"I'm ordering five thousand wristbands!" he yelled into the phone with a toothpick jumping around in his mouth. His forehead wrinkled as his eyes widened. "Well, heck, let's do it!" He called the kidney-transplant center, every hospital in town, and any person in the state of Utah he could talk into becoming a donor, and when he was not on the phone, he was still talking about it. He told me about all things organ donation and frantically gasped for air in between sentences.

"I'm going to solve this crisis by getting every person in the United States to be a donor! Every single person!" He pounded the steering wheel. "The party I sponsored was a hit! I called it Celebrate Brandon Curtis Day! There was a bounce house, tons of balloons, and food! We invited all the kids from his high school and signed them up to be donors! We broke the Guinness Book of World Records for the number of donors signed up in a single day!"

I listened in forced silence since he left no room for pauses or commentary of any kind. On his way out of the car, he continued talking loudly about saving lives. I picked up the car keys he had not even noticed he dropped and grabbed a grocery cart for him.

"Okay, Dad, what do you need?"

"It's not about what I need! It's about what they need!" he shouted.

We walked toward the refrigerated section and looked over the milk. A man walked past us, barely brushing my dad's shoulder. "Hey, hey, hey! Don't touch me!" Dad screamed.

I patted him on the back. "It's okay, let's get this one."

I put a gallon of milk in the cart and tried to direct him to an aisle that was not as crowded, a difficult task to accomplish when it only took one person to freak him out. Whenever people bumped him or came close, he screamed. Right alongside this powerful mania that was taking over his life was exhaustion and frustration. It was in those moments I saw the frustration in him dying to get out. He acted

like a caged animal. He bumped his way into other aisles of the store
and added bread, eggs, and cheese to the cart.

"Don't touch me!" he yelled at a woman reaching for a box of rice
next to him.

"Sorry," she apologized.

"All right, Dad, let's go." I carefully put my arm through his and
got him out of the store. I didn't think he would last much longer in
a crowded space.

"We need to drop these off to the Gomez family," he said, tossing
the bags of groceries in the car.

"Okay, I'd love to meet them," I said, buckling my seat belt.

We drove until we reached a small apartment building; he pulled
over on the side of the road and pointed to the door on the right.
"That's the one." Three new bicycles lay in the front lawn.

"David!" The mother of the three kids came out of the garage. She
smiled big and waved for us to come in.

"This is my daughter Sonja," he introduced me. She smiled wider
and shook my hand.

"Carmen," she said, placing her hand on her chest.

"Nice to meet you, Carmen." I smiled back. The grocery bags
swung side to side as we walked into her house.

"These are for you!" My dad set the bags down on the counter.

"Oh! Gracias! Gracias!" She set two cups down and poured us
some juice.

My dad finished his juice in one breath and slammed the cup on
the counter. "That's it! I've decided to pay for all three of your kids to
go to college!" he yelled. "Don't say anything!" He held up his hand to
Carmen. "It's happening!"

I about choked on my small sip of juice.

"And cars for everyone!" His eyes glowed.

"Dad, you can't afford that," I whispered.

"Shh!" He elbowed me. "You're just jealous."

Carmen seemed very nice, but there was no way he could afford
all of this. Don't let the giant mansion fool you; my dad was completely broke and in mounds of debt. I silently watched him make big
plans with Carmen and her boys; he was being so sweet and seemed

genuinely excited to be helping them. It was clear the Gomez family viewed my dad as their hero and an answer to many prayers, and maybe he was, in some ways, but he was making promises he couldn't keep; he just didn't know it. On our way out, I stopped him before getting in the car.

"Dad you're not thinking straight. You have to know your behavior's been a little crazy."

"I've thought about it. Am I crazy or are you all crazy? Because I know I'm not crazy, so it's gotta be all of you!"

His blue eyes were like marbles, leading to a hollow core. My dad was gone. The illness had taken him to a faraway place from where I could not rescue him. Was everything catching up to him? He had dealt with an abusive childhood, legal battles, financial stress, fatherhood, marriage, my mom's dozens of hospitalizations, his illness, medicine, and obsessions. He had so many cracks—how could he possibly keep repairing them until the dam was permanently breached? He was bleeding out with no protection left. I had never seen a living person's body missing their soul until that day. I took a close look at my dad's face, knowing he had to be somewhere in there, but all I saw was illness, and it scared me. The thought that our disease was strong enough to do that struck me with a new fear. I could go that crazy and not know it. I felt nothing but compassion for him, and I had to get him out of this. I hopped in the driver's seat before he could.

"Dad, get in the car." I started up the engine, and he quickly scampered over to the passenger seat.

"Where're you taking us?" he asked, popping a new toothpick in his mouth.

"To pick up Mom and then to your psychiatrist appointment," I answered, knowing he wouldn't like it.

Three minutes into the drive my dad started pretending to sleep. It was painfully clear he was faking, but he thought he had me fooled, like a child with a cookie behind their back. "I don't think I can make it." He reclined his seat back and started to cough. "I don't feel well," he said, peeping one eye open to see if I was watching him. My mom stayed quiet.

"Dad, we're going." I turned into the parking lot, and he stumbled his way out of the car, keeping up the sick act. I'm not sure what sudden sickness would cause a grown man to lose his ability to walk, but apparently, he had it. I put my arm around him and helped him into the waiting room. He slumped in one of the chairs, pretending to snore until his name was called and I forced him up.

"Hello, David," the psychiatrist greeted us. "So, who's this, another daughter?" Since most of my siblings had already tried to admit him, this psychiatrist had seen a lot of us lately. My dad kept his eyes closed and hung his head to the side, pretending to be sick or asleep; it was becoming unclear which one.

"I'm assuming you, like the rest of your family, want to admit him to the hospital. But I'm not convinced he's a danger to himself." The psychiatrist shrugged.

I bit my lip in a fury. "The very fact that all the people closest to him have been asking you to hospitalize him should be convincing enough, but if you're going to need another family member to say it, then read my lips." I raised my voice. "He *is* a danger to himself and others, so hospitalize him!"

"We can admit him and see if that changes anything, but I wouldn't bank on it."

"No! You can't do that!" My dad jumped up, miraculously awake.

"Yes, we can," the psychiatrist assured him.

My dad frantically dug around in his pocket for a phone, and in no time at all, he was talking to his lawyer. "They're trying to lock me up against my will. They can't do that!" he shouted.

We walked to the ER, where doctors and a security guard waited for us. We went into a room, and the doctors asked my dad some questions. My dad was not very honest when answering, so I clarified, but whenever I would talk he'd hush me, quite loudly. The last doctor left, and my dad and I were alone in a room with a security guard.

"Don't turn on me. Just go with what I say," my dad whispered. I ignored his comment and pulled out the bag of caramel popcorn I had brought, which was one of his favorite snacks.

"Here." I handed him the popcorn, and for the first time that day he got quiet. He held the small bag of Carmel corn in his lap and popped a few pieces in his mouth.

"What's your name?" he shouted to the security guard, crunching. "Hey! What's your name?" he shouted louder, but the guard ignored him. "You got a family?" He threw popcorn at him. "Hello?" The popcorn bounced off the guard's stiff uniform and rolled on the ground. "Helllooooooo?" He threw another piece of popcorn at the guard.

My dad was a wounded person falling apart. Deep down I knew he had fought the fight of a lifetime; he had this illness his whole life, undiagnosed, unmedicated, with no therapy, until just recently. And now the illness was taking over, and it was winning. When I was growing up, no one knew he had bipolar disorder. My siblings and I just thought our dad was unique and eccentric. That was our dad— that was all we knew. It was our normal. And like any child, we loved him with our whole hearts. It wasn't until he attempted suicide in his late sixties that he got diagnosed and we wondered if his big personality might have been caused by this illness.

The doctor came back in. "David, we're hospitalizing you."

"Look, I'll go to the psych ward if you just give me a little corner with a desk, a phone, and pad of paper so that I can get on with my work," my dad informed the doctor.

"We can't give you that."

"I'm saving lives through organ donation, and the work can't stop!" He stood up.

"We'll see what we can do." The doctor said trying to calm him down.

"Let's go." The security guard finally spoke to my dad as another security guard joined him.

"Don't touch me!" My dad yanked his arms away from the guards. The guards dropped their hands but walked tightly next to him down the hospital hallway.

"What type of daughter turns on her own father?" His tone turned sharp. "Everyone hear that?" He shouted to the nurses and doctors he passed. "My daughter turned on her own father!" He spat.

"I love you, Dad," I pleaded.

He flailed around, trying to turn and yell at me, but the guards kept him tightly facing forward as they walked. "I will never forgive you for this, Sonja. I hate you!" His scream echoed down the hall.

"I love you more!" I desperately yelled back, which is what he always told us when we told him we loved him. He continued walking out as though he did not hear me. Tears slowly slid down my face as I stood and watched my dad until he was out of sight. He never turned around. That would be the last time I ever saw my father. The look on his face and his words put permanent wounds on my soul that to this day still bleed.

# CHAPTER 29

# Shattered Faith

Forty-eight hours later, I woke up to a phone call.

"He's out. He's out of the hospital." My brother's voice rang through the phone.

"What, how? He just got admitted!" I panicked.

"It didn't matter. Dad talked himself out of the hospital. Mom is as mad as a hornet."

"So, I hospitalized him for nothing." I clenched my jaw.

"No, Sonja. You did your best."

I hung up the phone, and I locked myself in the only bathroom in our apartment. I pounded the walls, wanting to let out the loudest scream but ended up crying instead. The pain of hospitalizing my dad and not knowing where this illness would take him crushed me. I couldn't get the image of his vacant eyes out of my mind. They were like hard stones empty of any light. He was gone, and I wondered if I would ever get him back. This illness took so much.

What scared me most was that my dad was the strongest person I knew and if he couldn't survive his bipolar illness, how in the world could I? I put my head against the wall as the pain raged on.

I squeezed my eyes shut, trying to hold the tears back, but they escaped anyway, and I felt them slide down my face onto the bathroom floor. I let out my breath with a moan. I started to hit my forehead against the wall. Times like this I wish I could pay someone to beat me up. Hit me, throw me, and inflict physical pain upon me. After a quick reality check, I knew that wasn't really an option. But it still remained a temptation.

That night when Mitch came home, he found me in the safety net of my bed with my romance books. I had not left my bed all day. My books gave my head a place to be so I could block out unwanted thoughts.

"Hey, Sony." Mitch sighed. He sat on the edge of the bed to unlace his shoes. I put my book down.

"My dad's out of the hospital. I hospitalized him for nothing." My voice cracked as I tried holding back what few tears I had left.

"Oh, I'm sorry, Sonja." He reached out and touched my cheek. I looked up into his eyes.

"What's wrong? Something's wrong. What is it?" I asked.

"The recruiter called. I didn't get the job." He looked at me, not needing to say more.

In that moment, I felt God was cruel. My dad was back on a road of destruction, and now our life was in limbo. We had sold our house and were living in a two-bedroom apartment. What about the kids' schools and neighborhood we found in Lubbock? The recruiter said Mitch would get it! Then I was mad at the recruiter. Why would he lie to us and get our hopes up? How unprofessional! But then I was mad at Mitch—why did he need to move up in his career? Why couldn't we just settle for once?

"God must hate us." I swallowed.

"No, Sonja. The other candidate is God's child too. The job was meant for him and his family. Also, remember, when you had a spiritual impression we'd move in two years? That was seven months ago, so it hasn't been two years."

I had forgotten about that impression that had stayed with me for four days. Or had I wanted to forget it because I wanted Lubbock so bad?

I parked the car in a patch of loose gravel outside Mrs. Johnson's trailer park school. "Go on in, kids." The boys slipped out the back seat, and Rachael put her hand over mine. She tried to comfort me.

"Mom, I love you. Everything's going to be okay."

She looked at my red eyes with such confidence I wanted to believe her, but I couldn't shake my doubts. She shut the passenger door and went inside. I waited in the car, unsure if I felt betrayed or forgotten by God, and I wasn't sure which I'd prefer. I needed some counsel, and the wise old Johnsons were just a gray trailer door away. I walked in and saw Mrs. Johnson speed into her office to grab a pen. She was always on the move.

"Mrs. Johnson, wait," I called out to her.

She looked up and smiled. Mr. Johnson started making his way across the room.

"We didn't get Lubbock." I squeezed my lips together, trying to finish the sentence before crying. "And I don't know why." I put my hand over my mouth and Mrs. Johnson hugged me. She was only tall enough to hug around my elbows, but it was heartfelt.

Mr. Johnson shuffled over to me and patted my back. "I know this is hard, but God has something better for you."

"Nothing is better than the Lubbock job."

"You need to trust Him," Mrs. Johnson said.

"But, what if I don't want to trust Him? What if I'm just tired of it all?"

"Sometimes life is like a puzzle. All you see is a bunch of pieces that don't look like anything, but slowly, one by one, as you put it together, you see the beautiful picture God created in your life," Mrs. Johnson reassured me.

"You'll see, things will work out. Have some faith." Mr. Johnson rested both hands on his cane and nodded at me.

As sweet as his advice was, I could not take it. He said to have some faith, but that was the exact thing that had failed me. I had faith the doctors would help my dad. I had faith that we would get Lubbock and sold our house. I had faith that things would work out, and because of that faith we ended up crammed in a two-bedroom apartment with no prospects of moving, and my dad was out of the hospital. My faith was dried up, and in my spiritual drought, I did not want to pray for rain.

## CHAPTER 30

# A Step Toward Temptation

**W**hen were you going to do it?" Rachael yelled at me.

"Do what?" I set my phone on the kitchen counter.

"*Kill yourself!* Today, tomorrow, next week?"

Crap, she had found my letters on the computer.

"Rachael." I reached my hand out to comfort her.

She pushed my hand away. "When?" Her eyes filled with tears.

"I don't know," I answered honestly.

"You'd really leave us?"

"I—"

"Who'd take care of us when you're gone? It's selfish." She sat on the ground with her arms on top of her knees. "Does Dad know?"

"Not about the letters."

She looked up. "But does Dad know what you want to do?" Suicide was an unspoken word in our home, though it was referred to often.

"Yes, he knows." Mitch would often take my medicine to work with him to prevent me from overdosing.

"You didn't even write him one." She gritted her teeth.

"I was going to. Rachael, look at me." I waited, but she stayed focused on the cat next to her. "Look at me," I said more sternly.

"What?" she snapped.

"Rachael, they're just letters. I don't have a plan. I don't want to leave you, your brothers, or Dad. Ever. I'm still here because of all of you. It just gets so painful that I don't think I can do another moment. I wrote them in one of those moments. But, I'm still here." She cried into her arms, gripping the sides of her jeans. I sat down next to her. "Rachael, I love you."

"Then don't leave! If you really loved us, you'd stay!"

"I'm going to fight to stay with you guys. There's no doubt about that." I hugged her.

Although my suicidal feelings were no secret to my family, Rachael finding my suicide letters made it real. I had talked about suicide but never acted on it, never turned those thoughts into something tangible. I had taken a step toward my greatest temptation, and that scared me.

# CHAPTER 31

# Merry Christmas, Dad

Our small apartment did not require much to look filled with Christmas decorations. We put up a plastic tree and three stockings on a wall. Wrapped presents surrounded the tree. I kept my tradition of wrapping the kids' favorite cereal and a box of Capri Sun drinks. Those gifts were all we could fit under the tree before running out of space for other things, like a hallway. On Christmas morning, I called my dad.

"Merry Christmas!" I cheerfully announced.

He didn't respond.

"Are you there?"

"Yeah," he solemnly said.

I could feel the distance, but it was more distance than just what separated our two states. I knew even if I were in Utah, we would still feel all 1,223 miles between us. Allyson told me he spent his days sitting in his La-Z-Boy chair staring at the wall, detached from everyone and everything. The Opa that adored his grandkids wasn't present enough to so much as greet them when they came to visit.

"Dad, you just don't seem happy. What's going on?" I was met with more silence. He was spending his time up in his thoughts, detached from everyone. "Please just tell me what you're thinking."

He finally opened up. "You all think I need medicine because I'm crazy."

"Do you think your behavior has been a little crazy?" I carefully asked.

"It doesn't matter what I think at this point. I embraced who I thought I was, but you all rejected me." My dad's passion was an essential element of his personality, and he was lost without it.

"No, Dad, we're not rejecting you. We just want you to be healthy and happy."

"That's not a choice anymore. Being on medicine makes me hate my existence. I'm not myself. I can't experience anything. I'm doing this for your mother. I'm a model citizen now. I can't feel anything —no passion, no energy. All I feel is flat. I don't even know who I am anymore."

"You need to get a new doctor, Dad. You're overmedicated."

He did not respond. He seemed resigned to the idea that there were only two extremes he could live within: his manic side that turned his zest for life into an unmanned forest fire, or a medicated life completely snuffed of energy. And I wasn't sure which was worse.

"I love you, Dad."

He stayed silent. He still had not forgiven me for hospitalizing him.

"Dad?"

"Merry Christmas, Sonja." He hung up.

# CHAPTER 32

# The Phone Call

On February 8, 2011, I sat with my kids at the dinner table, staring at warmed-up Stouffer's lasagna. Mitch's conversation with the kids turned to white noise, and I felt indifferent to the world around me. Mitch's phone rang.

"Hello." He got quiet and then handed me the phone. "It's your sister Heidi. She needs to talk to you."

"Sonja, Dad's dead. He shot himself."

I dropped the phone.

Mitch swooped in and picked up the phone. "Heidi, we'll call you later."

I fell to the floor and let out a terrifying scream. *"No, No, No, No!"*

"What's wrong, Mom?" Rachael asked, frightened.

"He shot himself!" I cried out.

"Who?" Alex asked.

"Opa. Opa shot himself." I was too shocked to say it more delicately for my children.

The kids went silent. Their superhuman, horse-loving partner in crime was gone. He created a magical world for them and then completely shattered it. Rachael cried, and the boys were less sure how to express their loss.

No one tells you about the gruesome details of suicide. The specifics that all those involved are left with once they die. Like how my dad told a family friend he needed to borrow his gun to go rabbit hunting with his grandkids, which he instead used to end his life. Or how when my mom called, he asked her to stop and pick up some food before coming home so that he would have enough time to carry out his plan before she arrived. He took off his watch and placed it on the kitchen counter alongside his wallet with a note that read, "Time to go home." Or that my mom frantically searched the house looking for him, only to find him in the garage in the back seat of his car, dead, and the receipt for the bullets in the front seat.

What about my mom's bloody handprints that covered the walls and phone after she went from checking for my dad's pulse to dialing 911? Or how my brothers handled the police and my dad's body and the cleanup? We never talk about these things, but I wonder, how does someone let go of those moments before sleeping at night?

His death that day affected seven children, twenty-seven grandchildren, and his wife. My mom sat in a house without her husband for the first time in forty-nine years with those images burnt inside her being. I don't know about her private moments, but I never saw her crack, not once.

In this collision of tragic events, I was sure my injured heart would not beat another day. But somehow, I found myself dressed in black, sitting in a window seat, on a flight to my childhood home. Mitch and the kids would fly out a day later. Two girls in front of me laughed and chatted before takeoff. I could not help but wonder if I would ever laugh again. My haunting reality boarded the plane and took a seat right next to me, and lucky for me, it was in a chatty mood. I sat while that haunting little devil filled my head with the facts. My father was dead. He would never call me again to take two hours of my time, or hug me in that belly-scrunching type of way that only he knew how. My life would no longer have summers outside watching him hold and study his hummingbirds, or hearing his voice reassure me that I was loved, even in my darkest moments. No more him embarrassing me in public or night games of Settlers of Catan, with him wearing his Settlers hat and T-shirt.

And what haunted me most was the last time I saw him, in the hospital, screaming, he hated me. Why couldn't there be phones to heaven? I wanted to call and make sure he was okay. I wanted to tell him I loved him, and maybe this time I could hear him say it back.

I was on my way to a house where all his favorite things rested inside, archiving his life. I sat with my book up to my face during the whole flight to Utah, trying to hide from the people sitting next to me. I could feel a deep throat sob surfacing as tears hit the page.

"Must be a good book." The woman next to me leaned over, trying to peer at the cover.

I ignored her and slid my window cover open to view the tall, beautiful mountains of Utah. I started silently praying. *Dear Heavenly Father, this is Your daughter, Sonja. Please help! Will my life ever get better?* The plane rumbled as the wheels touched the runway. Holding my bag in a line full of people about to exit the plane, I felt a hand touch my shoulder. I turned and saw an older gentleman.

"It will get better," he gently said to me.

"Thank you." I nodded, acknowledging his kindness. God had answered my prayer through a complete stranger.

Heidi was waiting for me at baggage claim with her arms wide open. When my mom was pregnant with me, Heidi told everyone that she was getting a baby sister for her birthday. Everyone just laughed, thinking she was a silly four-year-old, but she was right. On her birthday, March 15, I was born. She always told me I was the best birthday gift she ever received.

The second I saw her, I sprinted into her arms and broke down all over again. "I'm so sorry, Sonja." She had just lost her father as well, but here she was comforting me. Heidi had always been the glue to our family—the strong, rational, and stable one. I knew it was a heavy load to carry at times. Even though she seemed to always have it together, in my opinion, she was the most sensitive of us all. She pulled away from me and looked me straight into my eyes. "You can do this." This was going to be one of the hardest moments in our lives, and I was so glad I did not have to go through it alone.

All my siblings were at the house; we sat on the couch together, comforting my mom, who cried but did not say much. I looked around and saw that every picture of my dad had been flipped facedown exc ept for one. It was a photo of his hands holding a hummingbird on his finger. I was positive my mom flipped them over because seeing him brought back the images of finding him that day in the back seat of his car. I hugged my mom and wondered how she was holding it all together. Her strength never ceased to amaze me.

Everyone sat around talking, but I heard nothing. I was silent in this surreal moment in time that I wasn't sure I could handle.

"I'm going to bring my bags up. You want to come?" Allyson asked.

Without saying anything, I picked up my bag and followed her. We walked up the tall curved staircase and past our parents' bedroom. The pain hit me hard, like the house itself was causing it. I turned and walked into my parents' bedroom.

"Allyson." I stopped and cried. "I can't do this."

"Yes, you can." She hugged me, and I stepped away from her.

"No. I just can't!" I screamed.

I lay on my parents' bed and pounded the mattress. I was losing it. I felt guilty. I should have flown out again to see my dad and gotten him more help. I should have helped him find a new psychiatrist. I should have done something. I felt a bigger responsibility than my other brothers and sisters because I knew what it felt like; I knew what being bipolar and dangerously suicidal meant. Everyone could hear me downstairs, and they quickly came up. Allyson went through my bags and got my medicine.

"Take this." She handed me my pills with a glass of water, then got on the bed and held me tight.

"Get the horse bracelet!" I cried. The horse bracelet was a beautiful gold bracelet that my dad had designed. It had seven wild horses running off the sides and the word FREEDOM engraved on the inside. My dad loved horses, and I felt like he wanted the same freedom his horses always seemed to reflect. He wanted freedom from his illness, just like I did. Everyone knew gold bracelets were one of my strongest comforts, and tonight the horse bracelet housed the comfort I desperately needed. Allyson put the bracelet on my wrist, and my siblings and mother knelt around the bed for a prayer as I continued to cry. Mike, my youngest brother, prayed that God would help me feel my father's love and that I could find peace.

That morning I woke up to chilly winter weather outside pressing against the window. Mitch and the kids had flown in, and I might as well have been on the moon. I didn't interact with them; I wasn't able to be present at all. Mitch completely took care of the kids and allowed me to mourn in my silent, distant way.

I went downstairs to find Heidi at work on the funeral program. She took charge of the planning, and we all just followed along as decisions had to be made for a casket, flowers, and obituary to put in the newspaper. Allyson, my mom, and I went to the morgue to take the clothes they would dress my father in.

"If you'd follow me this way." The morgue worker motioned down the hall. He moved to the side, and we all approached my dad's body. His head was wrapped like a mummy's with white gauze. I reached out and took his cold hand. It didn't feel real. The tears started pouring down—not one of us could keep the tears back. One by one, each of us held his hand.

I noticed his wedding ring was still on his finger. My dad had always proudly told everyone he had not taken his ring off since his wedding day, and he vowed he'd be buried with it.

"Mom, are you going to take his wedding ring off?" I asked.

"He wanted to be buried with it on. He said it a thousand times," she responded.

"Well, he's not here. What's he going to do if we take it?" Allyson said.

"Mom, if you want his ring, you should take it. It meant so much to him. It can comfort you," I said.

"You're right. I'll take it."

My mom asked the morgue worker to remove it, and she slipped it on her middle finger.

The day of the funeral I tugged my feet into black heels. The cool February air filled my lungs, and I gripped Allyson's hand for support. The long line of people came up to give my family their condolences—people I've known my whole life—but I felt frozen. I stood like a statue as close family friends hugged me.

"I'm so sorry for your loss. David was a great man." Their words fell to the ground. I stared, unable to speak.

My brother's wife, Melanie, came rushing forward. "Thank you for coming. It means a lot to us," she said as she shook their hand for me. Melanie always kept an eye on me in social situations and filled in the conversation to save me if I failed to respond. She loved me despite all my oddities.

Large rose arrangements filled the front of the chapel. Two hearts looped together in red and white roses with a banner that read, DOUBLE DOUBLE SWEETHEART. That was something my dad always called my mom.

As I walked up to the podium, I passed my dad's closed casket covered in red roses. I looked out at the black velvets and silks filling the benches in an overwhelming mass of ruffled fabric. Like the rest of the audience, his casket was still and quiet, the very two things my dad was not, and a subtle reminder that closed casket permanently locked him out of my life. I bent the microphone down and let out a shaky breath.

"One of my favorite stories about my dad is when my dad's brother, Roger, applied to join the Operation Engineer Union so he could do construction work and feed his family, he was denied because he did not have a high school diploma. However, if he passed the GED test, he could get in. Uncle Roger knew he couldn't pass since he dropped out of high school, so my dad took the GED test for him. Roger's score ended up being in the top one percent in the nation.

"A short time later, Roger was surprised when he received a letter from the University of Utah offering him an academic scholarship. Roger kept that letter as a reminder of my dad's love for him."

All seven of us children spoke and paid tribute to our father, a father we loved and adored.

# CHAPTER 33

# Haunting Memories

I found myself back on a plane to Utah several months later. Moving trucks filled the driveway, and I shielded my eyes from the sun as I looked up at the brownstone mansion, my dad's creation. My dad had sat in the big field, where our house now stood, sketching his dream house for hours; everything about the house reflected him. Since he was gone, I felt it was unfair for the house to still be there, reminding us of him in such detail. I stepped over the pavement to my mom's garden, where the flowers sulked as their dry roots waited for water. Many things had been put on pause after my dad's death, and gardening was one of them.

One of my old high school classmates and her mother pulled up in the driveway.

"We're here to see the baby grand piano," my old classmate called out the window of the car.

"Park and I'll show it to you," I said, walking away from the dying roses.

My mom was selling almost everything, as she got ready to move into a smaller home. I walked them to the white room, where, like its name, all the furniture and decorations were white, except for the shiny black baby grand piano. This room was my dad's shrine to his family. Covering each wall were oil paintings of every child and their spouse. My parents' portrait hung above the fireplace as if to preside over his children's portraits.

My dad had a somewhat predictable routine if you were new to the house. Before the usual house tour, he would begin in the white room. Instead of hearing my old classmate play the piano, all I could hear was my dad's booming voice reciting the resume and accomplishments of each child and their spouse. At times he even let details like their GPA slip out, or facts like my brother-in-law's number one class standing in law school, or my brothers' acceptance into the University of Pennsylvania Wharton Business School. It was boasting in its most shameless form.

"We'll think about it," my old classmate said, interrupting my thoughts.

"Sounds good," I said, snapping back into reality with my dad's voice still ringing in my ears.

My mom and I stood outside in the backyard, looking up at the gorgeous Maple Mountain. The day was warm and sunny like so many days I had spent here before. I could see my dad chasing the grandkids, wrestling them on the grass, calling them over to the hummingbird feeders, and riding bikes on the tennis courts. I remember the barbecues on lazy Sunday nights out on the patio, sprinklers, water guns, and the secret passage doors in the house that kept the kids' curiosity for hours. The racquetball court downstairs held memories of me as a teenager practicing my ballet routine for hours. Voices and memories of the past haunted me in this place, and I could not wait to leave.

I slept with my mom in her bedroom that night, on my dad's side, and kept thinking he should be there instead of me. She silently cried. The balcony sliding door was slid open, and I could feel the mountain breeze swirl in the room. My dad loved his Maple Mountain so much. Maybe when I woke up, he'd be lying in his bed, reading the newspaper or talking on the phone. I stayed there all night, but he never came. I looked straight ahead and saw the beautiful stained glass window above their bedroom doors.

"I want it," I suddenly said.

"Want what?" my mom questioned.

"The stained-glass window. I'll pay to have someone take it out and replace it with plain glass." I felt a desperate urge to not leave it behind. My dad had designed this piece himself.

Going through each item in the house reminded me of the dad I no longer had, and it completely wrecked me. I was suicidal myself, and my dad killing himself did not relieve me of that. Watching suicide wreck my entire family made my own suicidal feelings so much harder to accept. I would not do that to my kids I kept telling myself. But, now that I understood suicide's toll, I felt a new intense fear: my illness wanted me dead. I flew home once again; only this time there were no fumes left to inch me forward.

I collapsed in my bedroom closet with the steak knife gripped in my hand. I hadn't cut in years. I knew I should not do it. But I needed it. Emotions hit me like a hurricane, flooding, drowning, and damaging my very soul. I tried so hard to hold them in, to stop them or at least postpone their arrival, but I could not control the emotional domination polluting my mind.

I hit my head against the wall and tried to let go of the knife. Pain ran through my entire body, and it felt like an electric shock, like a literal stinging sensation beneath my skin. No more! I screamed in my head. I quickly stood up and ripped my sweats off and sat against the wall. I took the knife and cut a long straight line down my thigh. The physical pain registered immediately, and I could take a breath. Relief—it felt so good, too good. A small line of blood ran down my leg. I didn't care. The emotions started back up, and I cut again. And again, and again, and again.

"Mom? Mom, where are you?" Rachael called down the hall.

I froze. The closet light flicked on. My swollen cried-out eyes looked up at Rachael. Alex stood a few feet behind her. His stare sent a dagger through my heart.

"Please go," I whispered.

"But, Mom!" Rachael cried.

"Call Dad!" Alex said. It was a phrase the kids had become accustomed to repeating. Mitch was the kids' 911 responder when things were in crisis.

"Just go!" I looked down at my legs, hands, and knife covered in blood. "You shouldn't see this." I grabbed my sweatpants and covered my legs.

"Here." Rachael held out a brown marker. "Use this. Give me the knife."

I looked up and met her eyes. Guilt and shame washed over me. I was a horrible mom. No child should see her mother cutting. I peered around the corner and saw Alex on his knees, praying. I felt beyond even God's help. Yet, there he knelt praying for his mother. I was sure I was going to hell in the worst sort of way. It took everything I had in me to hand Rachael the knife, but I had to. She left, and I sat holding the marker. I had wanted to take the knife and cut all along my arm veins, too. So, I opened the marker and slowly traced all the veins on my arms and hands.

Neither my kids nor my husband ever discussed the marker lines that I left there for weeks. In a defiant move, I wore short sleeves, not caring who saw them. I had always cut in places where no one would see. But these lines were out on display. I didn't know what caused me not to hide them, but they brought me comfort in a strange sort of way. People stared, but that had never stopped me from doing things. The pain continued, the suffering continued, but I made a promise that my children would never see me cutting again. For them, I never did it again.

I sat at church in Relief Society. (Relief Society was for women eighteen years and older; it is the largest women's service organization in the world.) The young girls in the church joined us that Sunday for opening announcements. A twelve-year-old girl with brown hair in braids, wearing a colorful skirt with cowboy boots, captured my attention. She reminded me of Rachael. I wondered if that would be what my granddaughter would look like. I desperately wanted to meet my grandchildren. What would their personalities be like? I wanted to give them all the love and confidence in the world, but that was years away, and with the type of pain I was in, I didn't know if I would last to meet them. Could I make it? That ever-present question plagued my mind.

I looked up and saw Sister Wright. She was seventy-six years old with beautiful white hair and wrinkled hands. It amazed me that people could make it that far in life. Elderly people fascinated me. I felt a hundred years old inside and was shocked when I looked in the mirror and saw someone young. I wished I was seventy-six years old, but I was a long way off from that and still had a lot of life to live before I got there.

"Peace is one of God's greatest gifts to us. Does anyone have an example of when God helped you feel peace during a trial?" the Relief Society teacher asked.

A young mom in the back raised her hand. "I had a trial and got a blessing that said the trial would be over soon, which gave me some comfort. And the trial was over two weeks later."

"My house was on the market for three months before selling. We were financially strapped, and that tested my faith like nothing else," another woman chimed in.

An older woman tenderly spoke. "When my daughter passed away, I thought I'd never be happy again. But the beautiful thing about Jesus's grace is that He can heal you even if your trial never goes away."

I had a hard time making sense why the range of trials people went through seemed to vary so greatly. I turned around to see the woman speaking.

"It's been a year since she passed and I can honestly say I'm at peace with it now."

I wanted to say that, but couldn't. My grief was raging on, and I was full of guilt that I hadn't done enough to save my dad. I envied this woman's peace.

A relationship with the divine was supposed to give people peace, and people who were receiving that promise of peace surrounded me, so why not me? I sat feeling like an outcast that didn't have a place among these women. I couldn't keep listening to people testify about the very thing I had lived without but always longed for. I swiftly got up and left the room. I took a big breath and let it out as I opened the doors of the church.

I walked to a bench under a big oak tree and sat down. I pulled my phone out and dialed my dad's phone number, knowing he wouldn't pick up but ready to be shocked if he did. The phone rang and rang and rang until it went to his voice mail.

"Hi, you've reached David Nemelka. I'm not at the phone right now, so leave a message, and I'll get back to you."

His voice felt so tangible, like maybe in that moment, he really was too busy to pick up the phone. I let myself believe he was out with the horses or getting a Diet Coke at the local gas station, but when his message ended and all I heard was silence, the illusion vanished.

I looked up and right in front of me was the Baton Rouge Temple, a place my religion believes is the closest to heaven you can get on earth. It was a place that brought people peace, or at least that's what I was told; it never worked for me. In fact, I avoided the temple. I would get so anxious when I was there, I would often have to leave. I went to the temple out of pure obedience, and after I had gone, I looked to heaven and told God he owed me those happy, peaceful feelings everyone talked about, even if that meant in the next life.

I walked across the lawn to the big white marble building. I reached my hand out and traced the engraved words on the temple wall, HOLINESS TO THE LORD. THE HOUSE OF THE LORD. I kept my hand on those words and closed my eyes, remaining hopeful that some of that peace might penetrate my sick body. I waited, but nothing happened. "It's okay, I understand," I told God. "You let illnesses carry their course in people's lives." I looked up at the temple's tall white steeple. "But I'm making a pact with You: before I ever try to kill myself, You'll take me out first. Promise me, God, that You would take me out before I would ever do something like that to my family." At that moment, I believed with my whole soul that suicide would not be a part of my life story. God would protect me from it—He had to. We had made a pact.

At times like this, when I was struggling, Mitch tried to be the buffer, the one that made the kids believe everything was normal.

"Sonja, come on, let's get you cleaned up and go to a movie," Mitch said.

"I'm not going." My cheek lay on my tear-stained pillow.

Mitch sighed. "Sonja, it's becoming unhealthy for the kids to see all this. Please just come."

"Go without me." I tugged a blanket over my shoulders and continued looking at a picture of my dad. "Go be happy without me!"

I knew I sounded dramatic, but I meant it. My family didn't need my somber mood hanging over them. Incessant crying seemed to be my new routine. Mitch knew he couldn't go anywhere without me because I was not stable. Leaving me meant risking that I would harm myself in some way and even if I didn't, he knew I'd hate him for leaving me alone. Mitch was often in a no-win situation. He came back in the room, and instead of lying down next to me like he usually did, he stood by the bed, not touching me.

"Something has to change," Mitch said to the floor.

"What do you mean?" I asked, lifting my face up to him.

He stayed standing by the bed. "We've got to get out of this two-bedroom apartment and move on. We just lost your dad; we can't lose you too." He exhaled, and I could tell he was breaking. "I can't keep living this way." Mitch turned and walked out. I heard the front door close behind him and the kids.

The challenge with mental illness and marriage is that people wrongly assume one person is healthy and one is ill, and the healthy person is always functioning at one hundred percent and should be able to make up the emotional deficits of the mentally ill spouse. But in truth, when one spouse is depressed, the "healthy" spouse is also depressed. When I was anxious, Mitch was anxious; when I didn't sleep, Mitch didn't sleep; when I was manic, Mitch lived in a world spinning out of control. In bipolar support groups, they call this "compassion fatigue," and I could see Mitch was suffering from it. The worse I got, the worse he got; we were linked that way.

I knew the kids needed to feel some semblance of normalcy. I couldn't expect them to stay in bed with me all day as I cried and worked through months of grief. I got out of bed and started earnestly praying out loud. "God, I'm losing my family. I have nothing left inside to give. You have to help me. I can't do this alone." I started burying my grief deep, deep in the abyss of my soul, never to be found. I wrapped my arms tight around myself and closed my eyes as God gave me strength. I felt pieces of my soul coming apart. For now, I would use these breaking fragments to provide me with just enough strength to save my family, not knowing if I would ever be whole again. I slowly stood and tucked my dad's picture away in a book to start the process of turning my ship around.

# CHAPTER 34

# The Wrong Religion

I found a realtor, and we bought an adorable town house in a planned neighborhood with walking trails, a community swimming pool, and workout facility. Our home was one of many that backed up to a large pond. We had finally moved out of the two-bedroom apartment, and I unpacked in record time. I put on a brave front that things were completely great. I showered, changed my clothes, took my meds, and kept an immaculate house.

Tennis came to a halt; it just didn't feel right anymore. Our entire tennis community was shocked. Everyone knew my boys put in insane hours with a mother who picked up thousands of tennis balls day after day. We put tennis in the background and started focusing on private schools. The kids wrote application essays and got letters of recommendation. The schools we were looking at were harder to get into than many colleges. Finally, the kids got accepted to a private Baptist school and I couldn't believe we were willing to pay $10,000 per kid to attend one year. That week the kids got ready for their first day at their new school.

"Mom, it's time to get up." Alex flipped the lights on in my room. He and Lincoln stood by my bed.

"Just fifteen more minutes," I whined.

"Ugh." He sighed and called, "Rachael, help me get Mom up."

"Let her sleep. Then we can skip school." Lincoln smiled mischievously.

"Yeah, you wish," Rachael said to Lincoln as she came to my bedside. "I'm just preparing you. You have ten minutes before you need to get up." She patted my head and skipped out.

Most moms wake up their kids, get them breakfast, and make sure they have everything they need before sending them off to school. My kids did not have that luxury. Many mornings felt nearly impossible to get myself out of bed, let alone the kids.

"Time's up," Alex sternly said ten minutes later.

"Okay." I rolled over and continued to sleep.

"Mom, please get up." Rachael gently shook my shoulder.

"I am up." Just the thought of starting another day had me wanting to dig myself deeper into my bed and pretend it wasn't happening.

"No, you're not." Alex crossed his arms.

"Mom, we're not leaving until you get out of bed. If you would just buy me a car, I could take us all to school," Rachael declared.

"Not happening," I muttered.

"We can't be late, Mom," Alex said abruptly and yanked the blankets off me. I slowly sat up and went to the bathroom to splash cold water on my face. That was my beauty regime.

Attending a Baptist school as a Mormon was a problem for some of the teachers and students. Lincoln's teacher gave him a C on a paper because he inaccurately talked about Jesus.

Later that week, Rachael's civics teacher asked, "Are there any Mormons in here?"

Rachael raised her hand. "Yes."

"Weird. She doesn't *look* Mormon," a student commented.

Her teacher shuffled and let out a groan.

Rachael tried comforting him. "Oh, it's okay, you didn't offend me."

He sighed. "It's not that." He paused. "It's that I have a Mormon in my class."

My children heard frequent pronouncements from students and teachers that declared they were all going to hell because they went to the wrong church, and by their definition, weren't Christian enough. When the kids would get upset at the prejudice they experienced, Mitch reminded them that there was only one being in the universe that got to determine who was Christian and who was not, and that being did not attend their school.

Every Tuesday their school had chapel, which my kids absolutely adored. They sang upbeat Christian rock songs with a live student band that was equipped with a drummer and electric guitarist. The students and teachers danced in the aisles, praising the Lord. My kids introduced me to all the songs, and we fell in love with the Baptist radio channels, especially K-Love. We constantly listened to them in the car as we sang at the top of our lungs about our Lord.

After school, Rachael and the boys would drop their backpacks on each side of my bed and hop on top of the comforter. My bedroom was our family room; we ate snacks, talked about their day at school, talked about life, worked on homework together, and watched movies there. It was the first place we all gathered. I was very present in their lives even though I didn't want to leave my room a lot of the time. My bed was my safe place.

Private school relieved me of my concern about my kids' education. Rachael's English teacher told me she was a gifted writer. Since she had dyslexia, being considered a talented writer made me feel like she had overcome something big. Her creativity was able to shine brightly through something with which she had struggled.

Alex's reading scores came back at college levels, and I got an email from his history teacher telling me how polite he was and how much he contributed to class discussions. I was in complete shock since Alex had struggled terribly all three years at public school, not only with academics but also with behavior. I was constantly meeting with his teachers and principal because of his disruptive behavior and poor test scores. He had even pulled the fire alarm and would have his classmates time him running around the room whenever the teacher left. He was behind in math, reading, and writing.

In second grade, he was the only student who couldn't read their Mother's Day card. In fact, Alex was not just bad at reading; he hated it. After two years of homeschooling with private tutors and me, he started becoming a good reader. I still remember the day I found him sitting in the playroom reading a book, *Eragon*, for the first time on his own. He was completely focused and finished the 800-page book in a few days.

Lincoln was also getting straight A's at school and was gifted at math, which we hadn't known. He received the Extra Ten Percent Award, which was given to one student who gave more than one hundred percent in their schoolwork.

I couldn't believe it. For the first time, all my kids were earning academic awards. Usually, it was the complete opposite. When you homeschool your kids, it can be hard to know if you are doing enough, so seeing all my kids succeed at a private school was a big relief. Nevertheless, we continued to have the PhD history professor come on Saturdays to work with them on their writing, and I continued to teach them study skills.

Time moved on as it always does, and days turned into weeks, and weeks turned into months. We felt settled in our new neighborhood, and the kids enjoyed their school. Our house was filled with countless pizza parties where my kids and their friends roasted marshmallows in our fire pit.

Lincoln branched out and joined the football team at school. One day while I stood waiting for practice to finish I could feel a spirit of goodness radiating from the woman standing next to me. I wanted to be her friend, I wanted as much light in my life as I could. I introduced myself. We talked and I soon found out that Carly Swanson was a Baptist missionary.

"Dedicating yourself to Christ is a beautiful thing." I warmly told her.

"Oh, are you Baptist?" Carly asked.

"No, I'm Mormon."

"Then you're praying to the wrong Jesus," Carly informed me.

It was not the first time I had heard this. It was becoming my new normal. I was told more than once from evangelicals in Louisiana that I was going to hell because I hadn't accepted Christ into my life.

And even though I had accepted him, it was just apparently the wrong Jesus according to them.

Carly gave me a loving, but concerned look. "Would you please come to our church this Sunday?"

"Sure. My kids love chapel and I would love to see what it's all about." I had no problem attending churches of other faiths.

That Sunday the kids, Mitch, and I went to Carly's church service, and it was everything my kids had described. The band music, the dancing, the preacher, the message were all very beautiful.

Carly and I continued to be friends. We learned all about each other's beliefs and realized how closely our beliefs overlapped but also areas where they did not. Carly and her family were leaving for Macedonia soon on another Baptist service mission. I was sad to see them leave.

Four days before they left, I dropped off the fluffiest white towels I could find with a big bow holding the tall stack together to say good-bye. I knew the one thing Carly wanted most was a set of big fluffy white towels; they didn't have much money, so expensive towels were out of the question. Carly thanked me and then said, "Sonja, I'm worried about you. You and your family are going to hell unless you accept Christ."

"I do accept Christ in my life, and so does my family."

"You believe in the wrong Christ. You need to *stop* being Mormon and come to the real Christ," she pleaded.

"I don't think I believe in a different Jesus. I think He is the same for you as He is for me."

"No, you're wrong."

I hugged her. "Carly, we just see things differently. Please don't worry about us. I'm happy in my religion, and I'm not leaving it." I looked at her. "I know you and your family are going to heaven because you are some of the best people I know. I don't worry about your souls. Please don't worry about mine."

"I do, Sonja. And I always will."

I hugged her one last time. Goodbyes were hard for me. They always made me think about my dad and how I never got to say goodbye.

When the kids were gone to school and Mitch was at work I would spend hours sitting on our couch, staring at the wall. While I blocked out most of my grief, the one thing I couldn't stop was my dreams. I dreamed of my dad constantly. In my dream, my dad and I would go to KFC for dinner like we always did and talked at home on the couch as he read his newspaper. I told him about my kids, and he told me about his horses. Toward the end of my dream, I would beg him to stay, but the dream always ended the same. I'd get the phone call from Heidi that he died. I secretly continued to call his phone number, even though it had been disconnected, but I still called, hoping he might just answer. It was a fantasy I wasn't willing to give up.

# CHAPTER 35

# Unresolved Grief

I have to tell you, I'm in a somber mood today," Dr. Pope said, starting our psych appointment. "I'm a little more on the sadder side than I tend to be."

"Okay?" I was confused as to why he was sharing that information.

"Because right before you came I was feeling really sad, I started thinking about you, and I don't know if I've ever seen your sadness—in terms of like tears and grief. I've seen a lot of your tiredness and exhaustion but no grief, especially around your dad's passing. Do you feel like you inhibit your grief?"

"No, I'm fine." I started to fidget in the chair, not liking this conversation in the least.

"Sonja, grief isn't something you can skip over like a song on your playlist. We call that inhibited grieving. You have to go through it. You can't shove it and put it away. It will bubble back up and demand you deal with it."

"I believe that if I bury it deep enough, I'll forget it's there."

"It doesn't work that way. Sonja, you need to start your grieving process."

"I just can't deal with it right now. It's not a good time," I informed him.

"Grief isn't something you can put off. You lost a loved one, your father, in a very dramatic way. I want to help you process this traumatic event, but you have slammed the doors and vaulted them so no one can even get near the event. Can you open the doors?"

"No. No, I can't," I firmly stated.

"Sonja, it won't work, it will burst through and cause more wreckage than if you would open those doors willingly."

I refused to answer. There had to be another way.

When I got home, I set a bag of Taco Bell on the counter and called the kids for dinner. If we weren't having frozen lasagna, we were having Taco Bell. The kids grabbed the paper-wrapped tacos out of the bag and sat at the table.

"Sony, can I talk to you?" Mitch asked, getting up from the table.

"Yeah, what?" I looked at him as we moved into the living room.

"I made it to the final two for a job in Columbia, Missouri. I didn't tell you I was interviewing because I didn't want you to get your hopes up. We fly out next week."

I was shocked and stunned, but in a good way for once. "Wow!" I hugged him.

Mitch ended up getting the job. It had been exactly two years since I had the impression we would move in two years. I often reflected on the fact that the Lubbock job came seven months after that impression. Had I chosen to listen, I could have saved myself a lot of pain and headache because I would have known we weren't getting the job. But here we were two years later, moving to Columbia, Missouri. This was the job, the place we were supposed to move, not just for Mitch's career, but our family. I believed I could leave my problems and pain behind, not realizing that the problems were not housed within the state of Louisiana or in my neighborhood, but within me, as I would soon learn.

# CHAPTER 36

# Moving

*Columbia, Missouri, 2012*

W e moved into our house under the June sun and comfortably sank into our new Missouri lifestyle. Every day our family had more reasons to believe the Midwest was a hidden gem. The man who stained our deck brought us blackberries from his garden. They were such a small gift, yet it felt he was giving me something so much more than blackberries. The neighbors made their rounds to welcome us into the neighborhood, and it was not long before my boys had an army of friends.

That summer Mitch took Rachael to Europe before she left for college. While they were exploring Rome's Colosseum and the Louvre in Paris, I was surrounded by a troop of teenage boys. Our house became the party house. I would pile all the boys in the car and take them to the neighborhood swimming pool, or let them have water fights in the backyard. The basement was consistently loud while my boys and their friends played games with a plethora of pizza and soda.

During the two weeks Mitch was gone I had begun eating less and less each day until I stopped eating completely. It was like my body lost its will to live if he was not with me. That summer I realized if Mitch died before me, I would be gone three months later. Soul mates don't do well without each other. Even though it felt like an eternity, Mitch did come back, and I sat snuggled in his arms while he and Rachael flipped through their slideshow of pictures.

"Rachael, the bishop told me there was a woman named Sarah at church, who has some learning disabilities and a mental illness. I told him we'd go visit her tomorrow. Are you okay coming?" I asked in the middle of the slideshow, stopping her at a picture of her and Mitch in Venice.

"Sure, I'm fine with that."

We soon knew Sarah better than anyone, and she became a person whom I adored. I had many people come up to me at church and tell me how good I was to be her friend. I simply responded, "No, I'm lucky that she is my friend." They would just stare, not knowing what to say. I felt people often dismissed people with mental illness instead of looking deeper to the person inside. I saw Sarah's beautiful fighting spirit that loved me fiercely, and I loved her right back.

Rachael and I read the children's version of the scriptures with her and took her to get groceries at the local Hy-Vee most weeks. She would take me down aisles of food, showing me the products like I had never been to a grocery store before. Whenever I went to the grocery store without her, the cashiers would ask where my friend Sarah was. We were regulars.

Every Sunday, I drove Sarah to church and we'd make our way to a chapel bench. The sacrament prayer was said while the whole congregation sat reverently for the bread and water, except Sarah.

"So, I brought some of my hair in a Ziploc bag to the doctor's and he said I'm *not* going bald, but I don't believe him." Her voice filled everyone's ears.

"You can tell me after," I whispered.

"You believe me, right, Sister?"

"Of course!"

Mitch looked at me, a bit uncomfortable that our pew was drawing unwanted attention. No matter how many times I explained it, Sarah would talk throughout sacrament meeting. I related to Sarah's inability to stay quiet and conform. Who was I to say anything?

Often when at dinner with friends or people from Mitch's work, I would just stare at the person across from me. No matter how many times Mitch kicked my leg under the table to get me to stop, I couldn't. When I talked I had a tendency to repeat myself, saying the same thing four or five times but in different ways. I had this compulsion to make a point and hammer it home over and over again, even if everyone already agreed with me. Sometimes Mitch would smile at me and say, "Sweetheart, take yes for an answer. I've been agreeing with you all along." I asked Mitch to give me a cue if I started exhibiting strange behavior in public. We agreed on the phrase "Did the kids call?" When Mitch said this, I could modify my behavior. So, Sarah and I understood each other perfectly.

# CHAPTER 37

# My Kids' Greatest Trial

When Rachael left to start her freshman year of college at Brigham Young University, I cried my eyes out. While she was gone, I had to keep her bedroom door closed because whenever I saw her room, I would start to cry all over again. Rachael was such an essential part of my everyday life. She was my best friend; we did everything together. She kept me laughing until my stomach hurt. Her zest for life brought me a sense of joy in my tortured existence. When I would complain, she'd be just as firm and patient as any mother would be with their child. Going through the weeks without her felt strange, but we talked on the phone every day, and I was happy to hear she was enjoying college.

Alex soon followed Rachael in graduating from high school a year early and left for Brigham Young University. The house felt emptier and emptier. Alex was the responsible one. He was the man of the house when Mitch was gone. He made sure doors were locked, prayers were said, and no inappropriate jokes were told or laughed at. Alex was the enforcer of order in our somewhat chaotic life. Although we could be a handful at times for him, his steady presence was a comfort to me.

After my two oldest kids left, I started organizing their bedrooms and found a copy of their college admission essays. The question from the admissions committee was: "Tell us about your most difficult trial." I began to read.

Rachael Wasden's College Essay: "My Most Difficult Trial"

My most difficult trial has been having a bipolar mother. Growing up, my mother's behavior was just a part of life. I did not realize the severity of her condition or how learning to deal with it could help me become closer to my mother and God.

One night I opened our apartment door and shut it quietly when I noticed everyone was asleep. I turned the computer screen on, letting a soft glow illuminate the dark room. The first thing that popped up on the computer screen was a Word document. Out of curiosity, I read the short paragraph. Barely comprehending the first sentence, I quickly reread it after I realized my mom had written it. It was a suicide note. All the years of my mother's disease came flooding back to me. The nights in the ER, the weeks in the psych ward, the fighting and depressive states where she would spend months in bed. Feelings of anger filled my heart faster than any feelings of sorrow could. While desperately praying that night to my Heavenly Father for help, I felt this overwhelming love, compassion, and understanding for my mother that I had never felt before. I learned that God hears heartfelt prayers and my faith had been strengthened. Although God has not taken this difficult trial away, I have gained a firm testimony that the Savior will comfort and sustain me through any of life's trials I have and will face.

Alex Wasden's College Essay: "My Most Difficult Trial"

The hardest thing I have faced in my life is having a mother with severe bipolar disorder. I didn't fully understand the impact of this trial on my life until I had the following experience. I had just gotten home from school when I found my siblings in Mom's room. The expression on their faces signaled that something was terribly wrong. My mother looked at me with an eerie calm and said, "What do you want of mine? I am going to die tomorrow and want to leave you something." This time it felt as though her illness had broken her. This time she said it with a chilling acceptance that shook my soul. That night we prayed fervently, like we always did, that God would help her one more time through this trial. She didn't kill herself that night and is still alive today. I am grateful for having this challenge in my life. I have learned from having a bipolar mother that God gives us tender mercies just as we feel that the very gates of hell will consume the ones we love. I have also learned that I will never give up on family no matter how hard my life or my relationship with them seems.

I held the essays to my heart and wondered what business I had being a mother. Unwanted memories flooded my mind. How many times had Mitch been at a work dinner while Alex held my hand as I cried for hours? He would patiently listen to all my nonsense with only a simple reply: "I love you." Alex would then finally coax me into taking my meds and gently tuck me into bed. And what type of mother makes her daughter sit down and write their will with them every time they thought they couldn't live another hour? I didn't want to believe that when my children were asked, "What has been your hardest trial?" their answer was me, their mother.

# CHAPTER 38

# My People

My friend group grew as I started taking two new people, Bob and Carol, to church with me.

Bob was a single old man with a wispy comb-over who spent all his time at the library on the computer. Every week I invited Bob to sit with us, but he refused. He would sit in the very back of the church all alone. After three months, he started sitting with us and never stopped.

Carol was a frail little thing who told the most elaborate stories about her life. One story was about her son, who was a police officer, losing his hand in the line of duty. Another was about her other son, a missionary in some remote place living off the land with his wife and three children. She would tell me about the letters he sent her from their island, explaining their latest adventures. I came to find out it wasn't true. I don't like to say she lied; I believe she told a story she could live with. The reality is she had no contact with her sons and had not for years. I'm not sure of all the ins and outs of their lives, but her sons had essentially disowned Carol.

Our little mismatched family took up a whole row in church, and every Sunday we made quite the scene when we walked in the quiet chapel. I would help Carol get into the pew with her walker while Sarah and Bob bickered the whole way to our seats.

"Just one date?" Bob pleaded.

"Never! Stop asking!" Sarah shouted.

Bob leaned over to Sarah. "I think we'd be good together," he whispered as everyone bowed their heads for the sacrament prayer.

"You're too old, and you need to brush your teeth. Your breath stinks!" Sarah huffed, hitting the end of her rope. The row in front of us turned around.

"Sorry," I quietly apologized.

After sacrament meeting, I went to Relief Society. The teacher that week was discussing the principle of tithing with the group of women.

"Now, the word tithe literally means 'tenth.' The tithe was an obligatory offering from the law of Moses that required ten percent of an Israelite's annual increase. Can someone please read Malachi 3:10 in the Old Testament?" the teacher asked.

A white-haired woman in the back raised her hand and the teacher pointed to her. "'Bring ye all the tithes into the storehouse, that there may be meat in mine house, and prove me now herewith, saith the Lord of hosts, if I will not open you the windows of heaven, and pour you out a blessing, that there shall not be room enough to receive it.'"

"In this scripture, God is promising us that when we pay tithing, He will not only bless us but open the windows of heaven and bless us to the point that there won't be enough room to receive it. Does anyone have an experience with paying tithing they would like to share?" The teacher closed her scriptures and looked up at the group of women.

A woman raised her hand and began talking. "There was a time when my husband and I couldn't afford groceries. Our kids were two and five at the time. But despite not knowing where our next meal would come from, we paid our ten percent. That next day—" She choked up. "Sorry." She cleared her throat. "The next day one of our neighbors brought boxes of food to our house. They said they were going out of town and didn't want it going bad while they were gone. I couldn't help but feel that was a tender mercy from God."

Several other women shared touching stories of unexplainable blessings happening after paying tithing. As I sat and listened to how God had swooped in to help the people who were staying obedient to His laws and commandments, I felt left out. I wondered if I was the only one God left hanging despite living what I thought was a fairly obedient life.

A dark-haired woman in a purple dress raised her hand in front of me.

"My parents had been members of this church for only two years when my dad lost his job. They couldn't find a way to pay rent, and so they went to the bishop and told him they couldn't pay tithing that month. He told them they needed to have faith and pay their tithing anyway. So, they paid their tithing. There was no magic check in the mail. They ended up having to go on church welfare. Sometimes that's the true test of faith. Going through it and trusting God even when things don't work out the way you thought they should." She paused. "That's the hard part of life. That's real faith."

I looked at her; she seemed familiar. Then I remembered we had met at her house on the Fourth of July; her name was Lorie. She lived on a hill and had invited people over to watch the fireworks. After Relief Society was over, I walked up to Lorie, who was talking to Stephanie, a super friendly girl I had been getting to know, and told them, "We all should go to lunch sometime."

"That sounds great," Stephanie agreed.

"I don't do lunch," Lorie firmly stated.

Her honesty took me off guard, and I liked her even more. She was going to be my best friend; she just didn't know it yet.

At the end of church, I started the rounds to gather all my passengers, and we piled into my Honda Pilot. As I started driving to drop Carol off, out of the blue, I said, "What if I just drove us all to Mexico right now? We just go without telling anyone!" One of my fantasies was to just up and leave without notice and see where life took me— no plan, no responsibilities, no illnesses.

"I can go," Sarah said.

"Can we stop by my apartment so I can get my swimsuit?" Bob asked.

"I don't have anywhere I have to be. I can go," Carol added.

I laughed. "I love you guys. Of course, you would be willing to go on an adventure with me without notice. That's rare, my friends, very rare indeed. I can't today, but maybe someday we can all go instead of our outings to church, lunch, and shopping."

Later that day I kept thinking back to Lorie's story in Relief Society, about how sometimes things don't work out but God wants us to exercise faith anyway. I felt like she was someone I could relate to, like she had some wisdom I could benefit from. I knew Lorie was going to be an important person in my life. So, I was determined to win her over.

I made a flower arrangement and dropped it off at her house. She wasn't home, so I left it on the doorstep. She called me that same day and asked, "I don't do lunch, but would you want to go to dinner with our husbands?"

That weekend we went with Lorie and her husband, Dean, to a local restaurant, Chris McD's. Candles lit the middle of each table. I looked over the menu, and I ordered an appetizer for dinner before the waters were passed out.

"I've got a joke for you," Dean announced. "Why was King Arthur's army too tired to fight?"

"Why?" Mitch and I asked.

"They had too many sleepless nights." Dean barely waited for a reaction before telling the next joke. "I couldn't figure out why the baseball kept getting larger. Then it hit me."

Lorie rolled her eyes. "Dean collects G-rated jokes."

When our entrees came, I ate two of the five Asian-style scallops and boxed the rest. Then I asked to see the dessert menu. After briefly skimming over the menu, I told the waitress I would take one of each.

"You ordered all six desserts off the menu!" Lorie laughed.

"That way we can all try a bite of each." I shrugged. "Desserts are kind of my thing."

"It's true. She has a chocolate cupboard at home filled with all her favorite chocolate," Mitch added.

"Some people drink coffee in the morning, but when I wake up, the first thing I eat is a piece of chocolate," I said.

"I love that! I want a chocolate cupboard," Lorie said.

Food is what instantly bonded us. I went out and bought tons of mini chocolates and gave them to Lorie with a note: "Now you can start your own chocolate cupboard."

Lorie and I became fast friends. I either talked to her or saw her every day. We went to the local frozen custard shop, Andy's, and got kids' cones before watching *The Real Housewives of New York City* each week. We would discuss the show in depth, as if we were watching some type of mind-bending documentary.

Getting out of the house was a constant struggle for me, so it was great when Lorie and I would run errands together. When we did grocery shop, we would do yoga poses as we put our food on the checkout conveyer belt. Lorie and I had many traditions, like regular pedicures at Wal-Mart or going to restaurants together, where I loved to make things up about myself to the waitress. Lorie and I talked for hours, and her wisdom never ceased to amaze me. It became clear that she was an answer to years of prayers. She not only strengthened me but also helped me in a million little ways to survive my days. Yet, I still wasn't ready to share my secrets with her.

# CHAPTER 39

# Cause and Effect

A s a sophomore and a freshman in college, respectively, Rachael and Alex both decided to go on church service missions and put their studies on hold. They would teach people about Jesus Christ and help with many community service projects. Rachael went to Berlin, Germany, and dedicated eighteen months of her life. She had to learn German while Alex went on a Spanish-speaking assignment to Philadelphia, for two years. In our religion, going on a mission was an exciting and celebrated event.

Although I was already used to them not being home, having them that much farther away and one of them in a foreign country made the house feel even emptier. But lucky for me, Lincoln was my most social child, and filled all the empty spaces of the house with crowds of friends. Lincoln was also my most sensitive child. That week I became aware of how being raised by a sick mother was affecting him when one of his teachers called me to come meet with her.

"Mrs. Wasden." She greeted me warmly, but I got a sense she wanted something from me. I just didn't know what. "I have to tell you Lincoln is a very unusual teenager. I called you in today because my students were gossiping about our Spanish teacher on Friday."

"Oh, I'm so sorry—"

She cut in. "Except Lincoln. Despite being the youngest in the class he stood up for a teacher he had no obligation to defend."

"I'm glad to hear that." I stood up to leave.

"Wait." She reached into her desk drawer and handed me a wristband. It was blue and said ROCK BRIDGE CARES across it. "One of our students lost his brother and mom in a car accident. Lincoln organized a bunch of students, and they raised money to have a memorial bench put at the little brother's elementary school by selling these."

"I had no idea," I said, looking at the wristband and then at her.

Her eyes never left mine. "How's Lincoln so aware of people's suffering?" she asked.

She waited for a response I wasn't willing to give.

"It's very unusual for someone his age," she pressed.

I had no answer to give other than because I, his mother, suffered, and I didn't want to admit that to her. I started to panic as I realized she wasn't going to let this go. "I'm sorry. I have an appointment. I have to go." I picked up my purse and abruptly ran out of her classroom. I knew Lincoln wouldn't tell her our family secret. Not one of my kids had told their friends about my illness. As far as anyone knew my kids had a picture-perfect family. It was our family pact. We never let people in, ever.

That weekend Mitch and I sat on metal benches for one of Lincoln's tennis matches. He had just made varsity for the doubles team, and he was only a freshman. While we sat waiting for the game to start, a woman in a white Nike hat walked up to us.

"Hi, I'm Connor's mom." She put her hand on her chest. "I just wanted to thank you for what Lincoln did yesterday. It meant a lot to us."

"Sorry, what did he do?" I asked, perplexed and a little nervous.

"My son plays on the junior varsity team, and the other top varsity players usually bully him. Yesterday, on the bus ride to the tournament the ringleader of the bullying started throwing food at him and had the rest of the varsity players call him names and throw food at him too. But when he handed Lincoln food and demanded he participate, Lincoln told all of them to knock it off and then proceeded to walk to the front of the bus and sat with Connor." Tears filled her eyes. "Sorry, it's just the bullying has been really hard on him and because of your son, they've left him alone."

"Thanks for telling us." I hugged her.

"Enjoy the game," she said, patting my shoulder.

I looked at Mitch. "Did you know about that?"

"No," he said with wide eyes.

For years, I had sat paralyzed by the thought that my outward suffering had scarred my children in ways they would never be able to recover. I had never considered that any good could come from all those raw moments until now.

# CHAPTER 40

# Say It Out Loud

Since our church consisted of a lay ministry, meaning we had no paid clergy, each member took their turn in church assignments. I was currently a counselor in the Stake Relief Society Presidency and that meant one of these assignments included that we speak once a month to different congregations. This month it was my turn and I had prepared a talk on trials, since I felt that was my personal specialty. As the congregation sang the opening hymn, a strong feeling came over me that I needed to share that my dad took his life. Everything in me rebelled against that thought. I didn't talk about those types of things, especially to a group of 250 people. I assured myself that nobody needed to hear it, and I, for one, did not want to share it.

As I got halfway through my talk, the thought *You need to tell the truth about your father* hit me so powerfully that the words "My father chose to take his own life" slipped right out of my mouth. I looked out at the audience and saw I had everyone's attention. "I have many questions and fears. But, I do have hope that Christ will one day help me come to peace with it."

After my talk, I jumped up and ran out of the building as if it was crumbling, because I was so uncomfortable that I had just shared something so dark and personal. I pushed the double doors open and was stopped by a woman chasing after me.

"Wait! Wait!" she yelled.

I let go of the door handle and slowly turned around. "Yes?" I nervously asked.

There stood a young woman holding her two-year-old daughter in tears. "My mother took her life three months ago, and I haven't known how to handle it or how that type of a trial fits into our church. Your talk was such a comfort to me to let me know I'm not the only one struggling with this type of tragedy." She pulled me in for a hug. "You were an answer to my prayers today. Thank you!"

I was stunned. I never wanted people to find out about my demons or that suicide was part of my family history. I thought if people knew, they would judge me. Opening up to people about my life in a way that could help them was a new idea to me.

On my way home I stopped at Lorie's house.

"Lorie, I need to tell you something, something that until today no one outside my family knew," I said.

"Okay," she said hesitantly. She seemed nervous, knowing I had come here with a clear assignment. We walked over to the couch and sat down.

"My dad didn't just die, he killed himself. He was bipolar. And so am I."

"Wow, Sonja," she said, stunned.

"I've struggled with suicidal feelings most of my life." I admitted.

"I'm so sorry." Lorie put her arm around me.

"It's all right. I just wanted to tell you."

"Well, I'm glad you did. Just so you know, I struggle with depression."

"You do?" I asked, surprised.

"I'm on antidepressants, and some weeks I still don't leave the house because of my social anxiety."

A light bulb went off. "Oh, the 'I don't do lunch' thing."

"Yep!"

"I used to be fat."

"You were fat!" Lorie yelled, shocked.

"Yeah, I have fat pictures."

"I need to see these pictures. I don't believe you."

"I'll show you."

"You know what's funny? The first time we went out to dinner you barely ate any food, and I thought to myself, 'Ugh, another skinny girl who doesn't eat,' but then you ordered so many desserts!" She laughed.

"Don't worry. I only took one bite of each dessert. My bingeing days are long over," I assured her.

As scary as it was, I let her into my fortress and allowed her a glimpse into my world of darkness. Some days I was shocked that she loved me despite it all. I had believed I had to hide my illness from people. Lorie gave me confidence that one day I might be strong enough to open up to the world around me. She became like a sister to me.

When Lorie's mother was dying of cancer, people came and took turns sitting with her for a couple of hours a day. On one of my shifts, her mother informed me, "Another thing. I don't want anyone taking my Christmas ornaments, I really like those." She spoke as if she was going to be able to take the ornaments with her.

"Don't worry. Those ornaments won't hang on any tree other than your own," I assured her.

"Can you bring me my box of chocolates?" She sat up. "They're in the fridge." I got up and put the small box on her lap. We each took a piece and sat together eating the small squares of chocolate. "I don't usually have a second piece, but Lorie told me my doctor said I can't gain weight. So, I guess I'll indulge." She reached for a second. I bit my lip and tried not to laugh. It was clever of Lorie to tell her mom she couldn't gain weight since she was always so concerned about it. I stayed at her bedside while she slept.

"Are you still here?" She yawned, waking up.

"Of course. I'm not leaving anytime soon." I held her hand. "Can you do one thing for me?" I asked her.

"Sure." She smiled.

"I don't know what happens when you die, but if it's possible, could you go find a David Nemelka? He's my dad. If you find him, tell him I love him."

"Yes, I'll do that." Her eyes slowly closed back to sleep. "David Nemelka. David Nemelka," she repeated.

Lorie's mother wanted to live as long as possible—she was always saying she still had so much she wanted to do. I watched her sleep, confused. Here I sat a few inches away from death, but death was taking the wrong person. She wanted to stay. I wanted to go. Yet I stayed, and she left. There was a time when I looked at death with sympathy instead of envy, but that was years and years ago.

When I was a freshman in college I taped dozens of paper hearts all over my grandfather's hospital room.

"I'm not afraid to die," my grandpa told me.

"And you shouldn't be." I hugged him.

As I left my grandpa's room, I heard a man in the next room crying in pain. I looked around. Did anyone hear it? The nurses were chatting around the front desk. Did they not hear it? I peeked inside the door and saw an old man laying in his hospital bed, crying in pain. I slipped into the room and leaned over his bed.

"It will be okay. You won't always feel this way," I whispered, taking his hand in mine. He kept crying. I started to sing to him like I would comfort a child. I sang one of the church songs I knew by heart.

Within my heart a welcome guest,
Within my home abide.
O Savior, stay this night with me;
Behold, 'tis eventide.
O Savior, stay this night with me;
Behold, 'tis eventide.
And lone will be the night
If I cannot commune with thee
Nor find in thee my light.
The darkness of the world, I fear,
Would in my home abide.

"Beautiful," he whispered, still crying in pain. I kissed his hand. I felt connected to this man's pain. I didn't understand the connection at the time. Later, I realized my own life would be full of pain and somewhere deep down I think I always knew it was coming for me.

# CHAPTER 41

# The Need for Control

I went out to visit my mom in Utah for a week, and she took me on a drive down memory lane. We drove past my old elementary school, high school, and our old homes. It should have been a pleasant experience, but I hated the drive. I hated seeing all the places of my past. I couldn't handle the memories that would pop up with each stop to an old neighborhood or street. My dad was a part of them all, and it hurt. My mom talked as she drove around and reminisced, but my throat was closed off. I looked out the window and wondered how she could revisit these memories and not feel the torture I did.

"One last stop," my mom said, cranking the steering wheel to the left.

We pulled into the cemetery, and I clenched my jaw. We pulled right up to my dad's grave.

"Come out and say hi to your father." My mom got out of the car.

I glanced at his gravestone and then looked away. I couldn't do it; I could not stand at his grave knowing he was buried underneath me. I still hadn't let myself accept he was gone. I wanted to stay hidden in the car where he couldn't find me.

I rolled down the window. "I'll just say hi from here," I told my mom as I watched her fill the vase of flowers with water. The grief I thought I had buried so deep started pushing back up, and the feelings I had toward my dad's death were crushing me.

"I can't visit my mom in Utah anymore. I'm never going back to that state again, ever," I told my therapist, Dr. Randall.

"Never is a strong word." He raised his eyebrows.

"I don't feel safe there."

"Sonja, most people feel the safest and most comfortable in their childhood neighborhoods and home. There is a reason you're feeling this way. Could it be your father's suicide?"

"I just can't. I can't talk about it. If I open that box, I'll shatter, and what would that do to my husband and kids? It's too risky. I'll never go back to Utah, that'll be my solution."

"That doesn't seem like a good solution to me."

"My father killed himself. What if I killed myself? Can you promise me I won't do it? Can you?"

"No, I can't," he admitted.

"So, don't tell me my solution isn't good. I have to protect myself and my family at all costs."

"Just because your dad's life ended that way doesn't mean yours has to."

My therapist clearly had no idea what he was talking about or what was at stake.

The next morning I woke up, and my brain greeted me by screaming, "You're a horrible person! You don't deserve Mitch or your kids! You're worthless!" I rolled over and put my hands over my ears as if that would stop the voices in my head.

*"Stop! Just stop! I haven't even done anything wrong today. Let me start the day before you start yelling at me!"* I fought back, but the feelings of worthlessness stayed. I felt grief start to seep in, and I jumped out of bed as if it was on fire. *"No!"*

I immediately called Allyson, my refuge. "What are you doing?" I asked.

"Making homemade bread from scratch and my specialty strawberry rhubarb jam. What about you?"

"I'm just at home. I feel like I can't do this another minute. My life feels impossible."

"Sonja, you have Mitch, the kids, your family, and *me*! You're important to all of us. I believe in you."

"At least someone does."

"Hang in there. It will get better."

"But when? It's been over twenty years, and things haven't gotten better. Do you have a date you can give me?"

"I don't know when, but one day things will get better. You have to believe that too."

"I just don't understand what God's purpose is for me. Is it to stay in bed all day? I'm accomplishing nothing. All I do is endure. Is God trying to teach me something I haven't learned by now? Am I just suffering for suffering's sake?"

"Those are some big questions you'll have to take up with God."

"Well, I want to know where the customer service desk for God is located. I have a lot of complaints and questions. I can tell you that! I will not be giving them five stars on my review."

Allyson laughed. "I've got to go run some errands. I'll talk to you later today. Have faith, Sonja. I love you."

Lincoln walked in from school and sat at the kitchen table. "Mom, I want to graduate early like Rachael and Alex did, and I want to make varsity singles instead of doubles."

"You can do those things," I told him. "We just need to make a plan."

"Can we do that now?" he asked.

I got a piece of paper and wrote out the days of the week and highlighted the free hours he had in the day. "During these hours you can do more homework and practice tennis. I'll call your counselor to talk about graduating early."

I lived on the phone for the next three days. I called Lincoln's school counselors to finalize graduation dates. I signed Lincoln up for an online math class on top of his current classes. Then I hired a tutor to help him study for the ACT, since that needed to be taken now that he was graduating early.

I called the very best tennis coaches and players to practice with Lincoln. Falling into full tennis mode felt like second nature to me after living and breathing tennis when the boys were younger.

Looking in the tightest of corners for something that resembled consistency and control, I typed out every hour of Lincoln's day and filled it math tutors, ACT tutors, writing tutors, tennis matches, homework, and any additional studying I could cram in. I left no time for breaks, and I made sure no hour was wasted. The Word document proved I had made something organized and filled with important activities. It was measurable proof that for all my faults, I was a great mother. I hit print and my masterpiece came out of the printer. I slapped the pages on the fridge with magnets. I showed Lincoln his new schedule.

"What do you think?" I asked him.

"It looks like not a lot of free time." He seemed worried.

"Hard work will pay off, and if you follow this schedule, you will reach all your goals by the time school ends!"

"I'll do it," he said.

That night, the painters I had hired earlier that week greeted Mitch. He walked around the ladder, his shoes crinkling on plastic drop cloths.

"What's going on?" he asked, confused.

"I'm having the whole house repainted," I said as if it was obvious.

"I thought you liked the color of the walls."

"Oh, I love them, the paint color is staying the same, but I saw a few scuffs, so we're repainting the house."

"This is a brand-new house! Sonja, you don't even let people touch the walls. They're in perfect condition!"

I gave Mitch a piercing look to communicate my anger at his questioning. If he wanted to go head-to-head with me in front of the painters, he would lose.

"Whatever," he sighed and went into the bedroom.

My obsessions from the paint on the walls carried on to the paintings that hung in my house. I felt a strong desire for everything to be perfect, so I could find some peace.

I marched through the automatic doors of Michaels craft store for the fifth time that week, carrying a large painting to get reframed. The framing section of the store started to feel like my office. I even had my own seat, the bar stool on the right side of the counter.

"Is Mark here?" I asked an employee.

"He's in the back. I'll go get him."

"Tell him Sonja's here," I shouted to her as she walked away. I didn't have time to start all over with a new employee. Mark and I had already had ten plus hours of conversation about this piece, plus I trusted his opinion, which was hard for most employees to accomplish. I pulled out the frame samples we had been deciding between and stopped anyone who passed me.

"Which one do you think is more gorgeous?" I asked, holding up gold and silver corner pieces to the painting.

"Um, I like gold frames." An older woman with a puffy hairdo hesitated. "So, I'd say that one?"

"But which one is more stunning?" I pressed.

"I don't know, maybe the silver?" She switched, thinking her first answer was ill-received.

"If you had to rate them, one out of ten, what would they be?" I kept my eyes locked on the corner samples and tried to answer the questions myself.

"The gold would be an eight and the silver a five," she said more confidently.

"Okay." I quickly turned to the next person. "Excuse me, which one do you think is prettier?" The young mom jolted to a stop and gripped her cart handle as she narrowed her eyes at the frames.

"Definitely the gold. Hands down." Her confidence got me excited. She sounded like she knew which one I should pick.

"Why's that?" I asked, still holding up the painting.

"The gold makes the painting pop and adds some class. The silver's nice too."

"But which one is more stunning?"

Mark sighed and walked up behind me. "Good morning, what are we looking at today?" I got back in my seat and laid the painting down in front of him.

"I'm still deciding between the silver and gold. Which one do you think looks best?"

"My answer is still the same. The gold."

I looked at the gold sample piece, studying it next to the painting as if it was for the first time, when in reality I had spent eleven hours in contemplation. I turned to the first employee I had approached. "Which frame is more gorgeous?" I saw Mark roll his eyes, but I felt we had to get to the bottom of this.

"I like the silver," she flatly responded.

"Really?" I was surprised. "Because Mark thinks the gold is better."

"Which one do you like better?" she asked.

"I don't know." I stared at the two samples that had started to blur together. "I can't decide."

"Ma'am, I need to help another customer," Mark said and leaned to the side where a man had been waiting for quite some time.

"Why do you like the gold better?" I desperately asked.

"Just because I think it looks better," he answered, exasperated.

"But, why does it look better?"

"It just does," he said, leaving me at the counter to go help the other customers.

I pulled up an employee chair, sat down, and continued to stare at the silver and gold frames, trying to figure out which one was more stunning, gorgeous, and unique. I continued to ask strangers for their thoughts on the matter. Six hours passed. Mark was fed up and got the manager involved.

"Ma'am, you need to leave. You've been here all day." The manager stood in front of me. "You're disturbing the customers and making it hard for Mark and the other employees to do their job. And this isn't the first time."

"Okay, okay, but real quick—which frame is more gorgeous?" I slid the gold and silver samples to her.

"Is there someone we can call to come get you, so we don't have to call the police?"

"You can call my husband," I suggested.

"Okay, let's do that."

"And maybe he can pick a frame." I lit up.

The manager explained the situation to Mitch over the phone, and he assured them he was on his way. When he got there, he gently grabbed my arm. "C'mon Sony, let's go."

"No, not yet. You need to see something first." I pointed to the frames. "Gold or silver?"

"We can worry about this tomorrow because today you need to leave the store." Mitch turned to the manager. "I'm sorry, she's not well right now."

The next day, I was back at Michaels as soon as it opened. I had my painting in hand and went to the framing section. Mark could not help but tense up when he saw me. I called Lorie and asked her to come help me choose a frame, but like everyone else's opinions, nothing would satisfy me. After Lorie arrived, Mark went and got the manager.

"We're going to have to ask you to leave," the manager sternly told me.

"How will I frame my painting then?" I asked.

"Please take her out of here." The manager turned to Lorie.

"Let me frame my painting first, and then I'll be gone, promise!" I frantically looked at the frames, wishing I could just choose one. "Just give me one second!"

"I'm not asking you to leave. I'm telling you that you can no longer shop here," the manager corrected.

"What? Wait. What about my painting?" I gasped.

"Take your painting *somewhere* else. We refuse to frame it."

I slid down on the floor and sat in confusion. "No, this can't be happening. You don't understand. I can't leave until a frame is picked out." I slid my hands over my head. "This can't be happening."

"Please get off the floor," the manager firmly stated.

"I can't."

"Don't worry, we'll get your painting framed." Lorie pulled me off the ground. "Sorry again." She waved to the manager.

A week later I opened the front door to find two of my favorite things: Lorie and my painting. Framed. The painting looked beautiful. She went with a light silver frame and white mat board. People often wondered how I couldn't see how obsessive I was being. My only answer: slipping into insanity's easy; it's coming out of it that's hard.

CHAPTER 42

# Searching for Solace

Lincoln had always been an obedient child and lived out the schedule for days and then weeks and then months.

"Your ACT tutor is coming in thirty minutes," I reminded him, tapping the schedule.

"Can I have a thirty-minute break then?" he asked.

"No." I shook my head, shocked he was even asking. "You have to finish your homework for tomorrow. When else will you do that?"

"Mom, nobody else is doing this."

"Good. That's how you get ahead in life. Outworking everybody else."

"You're being crazy! I can't do any more studying!" he cried as he hit his fist on the table.

"Well, we all have to do things we don't want to." I unzipped his backpack and dropped the books on the table.

"You're not listening! I'm exhausted! I'm literally done!" He screamed until my ears hurt.

My need to control something, anything, in my unraveling world was so intense I didn't notice he was cracking. "You have to follow the schedule. We aren't quitters in this family. These are *your* goals!

You want to make the varsity tennis team and graduate early, and this is what it takes."

"You don't get it!" He clenched his fists with tears in his eyes. He picked up his phone and threw it against the wall, shattering the screen.

"Lincoln! You're going to pay for that! Now sit down and get back to work! You have twenty minutes to calm down before the ACT tutor gets here!"

Lincoln sobbed for twenty minutes, picking up the pieces of his phone. When the ACT tutor came, he forced himself to look composed and sat at the table.

Conducting Lincoln's daily schedule gave me some sort of grip on my life that I otherwise didn't have. Even though Lincoln and I repeatedly fought about his schedule, I held onto it as if my very life depended on it.

Confused and depressed, I lay in bed with my laptop. I was watching dozens of jewelry items on eBay and kept a constant tab open for each of them. Today four of the items were ending, and like a bad gambler with nothing to lose, I bid high and won them all. A piece of jewelry arrived at least every two days. We had so many packages that the mail carrier would bring a bin stuffed to my front door. One day she asked if I ran an eBay business, to which I replied no and shut the door without further explanation.

For the last twenty years, Mitch had paid off my overspending, giving me an unbelievable credit score of 810. Every bank on the planet was happy to lend me money, and I took advantage of as many credit card offers as I could, even credit cards in Mitch's name without him knowing. It never crossed my mind to consider the stress I was putting on my family or the damage I was doing to my marriage, nor did I consider how I would pay the credit card companies.

As I dropped deeper and deeper into a full-blown mania, my jewelry addiction climaxed, as did my standard of perfection. Each piece of jewelry required weeks of mental deliberation and consultation with others. It felt like a piece of me would die not to have them. I spent hundreds of hours over several months on eBay; there was little time for anything else. My illness demanded perfection, and it felt like I was being dragged by its need for exactness. My mind was a punishing taskmaster.

I bought a pair of Brian Gavin diamond stud earrings, one carat each. They were immaculate, but shortly after getting them, I wondered if one carat in each ear was too small. My mind would not rest until I came to a conclusion.

Because I knew Brian Gavin was one of the best diamond experts in the world, I talked to his people constantly to seek their reassurances about my earrings' size, brilliance, and quality. In fact, I couldn't call enough, so I called with fake names just to re-ask my questions repeatedly.

"This is Hannah from Brian Gavin. How may I help you?"

"Hi, this is Margie. How would I know if my diamonds are too small?" I inquired.

"Isn't this Susan? I recognize your voice. You've already called."

I hung up and called back, hoping to get a different sales representative.

Although the diamonds were beautiful, the reoccurring thought that they were too small wouldn't leave me. I ended up returning them that week and starting a new and more challenging hunt to match my own set of three-carat earrings. I spent my days scrolling through eBay from morning till night. It didn't matter if the GIA diamond report thought they were excellent cut, or if the seller thought the two stones' roundness was close enough to be a match. I needed to get as close to perfection as I could. Toward the end of the third month, the stars aligned, and I found my two GIA-certified diamonds from two different sellers on eBay.

One was a diamond in a wedding band, and the other was a loose diamond. I bought the wedding ring and had the diamond removed. My only problem was that the other diamond's crown angle was 41 when it should be under 40.9. I needed to know if the GIA had rounded up, so it was really 40.9. I knew the GIA rounded up or down if it was close.

I once again called GIA headquarters and asked to speak to the department in charge of measuring the diamonds. I had them pull up the certificate on the diamond I wanted to buy, and thankfully they had rounded up. I could now purchase the diamond in confidence. Like an addiction, it was a cycle of momentary relief and constant craving. In three short months, I had amassed credit cards bills totaling over $150,000. I was out of control, and I knew it.

In my desperation, I met with my psychiatrist. I did not even give him the chance to sit down before I stumbled in and declared, "Doctor, help me! I'm on a runaway train. Not one of the medicines you've given me are working."

"Sonja, sit down," he said, trying to gain some control in the room.

"I've tried Lithium, Ambilify, Zyprexa, Seroquel, and Risperdal. They either don't work, or the side effects have been worse than the illness. I need real help!"

"Sonja, breathe," he said. "It can take years to find the right medication. Don't worry."

"I feel like I'm in the passenger seat of a car with my illness at the wheel and I have no say where we're going." I panicked because I knew he was not feeling the same sense of urgency I was. "I've spent 68,000 dollars in the last two weeks, and that's just on one of my ten credit cards!" I looked at him, waiting for him to wake up and see the dire situation I was in.

"People with bipolar disorder often have impulsive spending sprees in mania and are more at risk for being debt-ridden than the general population," he told me, as if he was conducting a lecture to a bunch of students.

I didn't engage with his classroom facts. In silence, I stared at him, demanding he see past my illness, to the person—me—in this body who needed serious help, not a debriefing on bipolar symptoms. He said nothing and looked away. I felt I had no other option.

"Lock me up," I demanded.

# CHAPTER 43

# Psych Ward

*The Roommate*

I was back in the psych ward, only this time it was by choice. Late into the night a nurse and patient barged into my room. "This is your new roommate." I looked over at the flailing woman to whom the nurse was referring.

"Stop that!" The nurse yanked her arms back. She was shaking and tried to use the zipper of her jeans to cut into her wrist. I sat silently on my bed, watching the scene play out.

"I know it's there," she mumbled. "I know it's there." She dug the zipper deeper into her wrist. She and the nurse got into a tug-of-war over the jeans.

"You need to stop this!" The nurse sat her on the bed and held her wrists tight.

"I want it out!" she screamed.

"For the last time" —the nurse gritted her teeth, and yanked the jeans from her hands—"we did *not* put a tracking device in you." She roughly shut the door on her way out.

My new roommate fell into the fetal position, threw her arms over her knees, and began to rock back and forth while she sobbed.

The resemblance was all too familiar to the thousands of meltdowns I had experienced.

That night was the first time I had ever seen someone behave like me up close. I cringed watching her as she shook and moaned. Was this what my children saw when I lost it? Is this the same type of broken person Mitch cuddled and attempted to comfort on a weekly basis? My eyes burned as I looked at her. My children—*my children*— had seen me like that. It must have scared them. How could I ever accept that *this* was part of the person my kids called Mom? I wanted to tell her to stop, to sit up, to get a grip and be an adult, but I knew better than anyone those things were not going to happen. I couldn't watch any longer. I got up and immediately walked to the nurse's station.

"I need to be moved to another room," I stated, firmly gripping the corner of the desk.

"We don't just change rooms, Sonja." The nurse scoffed.

"You have to move me to another room! I can't sleep with her. I can't be around her." I was starting to hyperventilate.

"Just calm down. Why don't we just see how it goes?"

I knew I was losing this battle. I stood in the hallway next to my room, unable to go in. Nurses were coming in and out administering meds and calming my roommate down. I was still shaking. I couldn't move. My feet stayed planted in the hallway as I leaned against the wall with my eyes closed. I didn't want more meds, so I resorted to deep breathing, although my breaths were fast and shallow at the beginning.

I talked to my Savior as I always did, pleading. I wondered if He ever got tired of my prayers. They were always the same. "This is Your daughter, Sonja, please help!"

I don't know how much time passed, but I slowly felt my heart calm down. I carefully opened my eyes and gathered all my strength to go into my room. I quietly walked toward my room, afraid of being surrounded by the reminder that my roommate was my mirror. When I peeked behind the door, she was no longer in a state of panic. Instead, she sat cross-legged on the floor and was wiping our bedroom walls with a T-shirt. I watched for a minute before I asked, "What are you doing?"

"I'm getting the blood off the walls." She didn't look at me and continued wiping. I looked at the wall and clearly saw there was no blood, but I also knew that she saw blood. It was her reality, and I was not going to tell her it was nonsense.

"Do you want any help?" I asked.

"No," she quickly said.

I lay in bed and listened to the cotton drag against the concrete walls, until she finally got into her bed.

"Did you get most of it?" I asked.

"Yeah, you can turn off the lights now." I got up to flip the light switch off.

"Good night," I said in the dark. She didn't say anything back.

The very next morning I was brought to my doctor and found myself in the middle of a rather lengthy session.

"Sonja, you need to stop fighting your illness."

"I can't," I answered, frustrated. I couldn't even get massages without the massage therapist asking me to relax because I was so tense.

"What is keeping you from—"

"It's not safe."

"Can't you stop fighting it even for a moment?" he asked.

"No. I feel like I'm going to explode—just blow up into a million little pieces. So, I keep holding myself together as tightly as I can. If I let go, I may make even worse decisions."

He looked at me and leaned forward. "You have to let some of it go. You need to pull yourself out of this episode, Sonja."

"I'm fully aware I have to pull myself out of this, but I don't see how relaxing into this deep pit I've dug for myself is going to help me get out of it. I'll have to claw my way out inch by inch and stay in control."

"What do you think will happen if you lay down some weapons and take a break from fighting your illness?" he asked.

"I don't know for sure," I admitted.

"Exactly. So, why not try?" he suggested.

"But what if I lose it?" I looked up at him, scared.

"But what if you don't, and it makes it easier?"

"It's just safer to resist."

"Is it?"

"It seems so." I shrugged.

"From where I'm sitting, it doesn't look like that's worked out for you."

"Well, I'm still alive, aren't I?"

"Can't you let go for just a second? We can try the experiment right now."

"You don't know what you are asking me to do!"

"Yes, I do."

"Oh, really? To end up dead like my father? To go completely *crazy*? I'm already somewhat crazy, but I refuse to be utterly *gone*!"

"You don't know that will happen."

Even though the doctor was the one with the degree, it was hard not to feel like he had no idea what I needed or what was at stake. It felt like he was asking me to give into the illness, the very thing I was fighting to avoid every day.

"I don't need to relax into this illness to know it's going to kill me. I've already seen what giving in or getting lost in this illness looks like through my dad's life, and that's not a scenario I'm going to watch play out in mine."

"What you are doing is making your pain worse."

"Do you have any clue how scary it is to have some days when the thought of going out like my dad paralyzes me, and other days when it sounds like a seducing reality? And on those days, I'm scared of myself because of how much I want it."

"Have you heard the story of the Bear?"

"Yes. He grabs hold of a burning stick, and instead of letting go, he holds on tighter, trying to get rid of the pain," I mumbled.

"Exactly, when all he had to do was let go of the burning stick and the pain would stop."

"So, if I let go, my illness will be separate from me? The problem is it's in me, and there is not a doctor on this planet that can cure me. Do you hear me? *Incurable*!" I got up to leave, I was so angry.

He stopped me. "But not untreatable. We'll put you back on Geodon. That medicine helped get you out of a manic episode last time."

I needed to calm down. I walked out and saw everyone going to activity time. The tables were filled with magazines and glue sticks. I sat at a table and picked up a magazine.

"What is the activity today?" I asked my neighbor.

"We're making collages of things that we like," he responded.

I thumbed through the magazine and saw lots of vacation spots I wanted to put in my collage. "Can you pass me the scissors?" I asked the woman sitting next to me.

"We don't have any. The nurse said to tear them out."

I attempted to tear out a small picture of Bora Bora. The paper tore in the wrong direction, leaving me with half a grass hut on the beach. I rolled my eyes and threw the picture away. Everyone around me seemed to be enjoying themselves, gluing poorly ripped photos of puppies and cars onto their paper. Luckily, I loved reading magazines, and they had my favorite there, *People*. I grabbed two *People* magazines and read outdated celebrity news for the rest of activity time.

"Everyone line up for meds!" the nurse shouted.

I got in line behind my roommate, Amber. She looked at me like she saw a ghost; she always looked terrified. Amber was skittish around people, so she backed away from me and stood a few feet outside the line. She started shaking and trembling. I knew that meant she was on the verge of a panic attack. I looked at the nurse administrating medicine.

"Can Amber get her meds next? She needs them."

The nurse looked up at me and then at Amber. "No, she needs to wait her turn. There are a lot of people in front of her."

Frustrated, I turned to the other patients in line. "Do any of you mind if Amber cuts the line so she can get her meds next?"

"No," a few people around us said. The other people moved out of the way for her to go ahead of them.

"All right, Amber, come on up." The nurse waved to her.

Amber went back into our room after getting her meds, and I went in after I got mine. Amber was lying in her bed on her side.

"You okay?" I asked her.

"Yeah. Thanks for that," she said, still facing the wall.

"No big deal." I shrugged.

"I'm in here because I always see people bleeding from bullet holes. My life is like a horror movie."

"Have you seen me like that?" I asked.

"Yes, everyone looks like they're injured and bloody to me. I never know what's real and what's not."

"That must be really scary. I'm sorry, Amber."

"When I was admitted to the ER I tried so hard to escape; I heard voices telling me if I didn't leave immediately they would blow up the hospital. I didn't want anyone to die. I was trying to save them."

"It was kind of you to try to save everyone. You're brave." I said.

She turned and looked up at me. "No one has called me brave before. People usually just think I act strange."

"Anyone who saw what you see would act strange. I would be more concerned if you saw bullet holes in people and weren't terrified. So, you're actually very normal."

"Ha, I've never thought about it like that. But you're right." She smiled.

"If you could trade your illness with someone, would you?" I asked her.

"No, I wouldn't want anyone to have this." She shook her head.

"Really? You wouldn't be tempted to get rid of it, even a little?" I was shocked.

"No, no, no. I wouldn't be able to live with myself if someone else had this because of me. I've been in and out of psych wards since I was ten, so I've gotten good at handling this."

"You're better than I am." I sighed. "If I could trade my mental illness away, I would. I'm not as kind as you are. God's proud of you."

"I don't know much about God, but you think He would be proud of me?"

I reached my hand out, and she took it. "I know for sure God is not only proud of you, but He loves you and is aware of you."

Tears started to fall onto her pillow. "Thank you."

"Sonja, the phone's for you!" a woman in her forties with thick scars all up her arms from cutting cheerfully called into our room.

"Thanks," I muttered, getting up from my bed. I was astonished that woman was a patient here. She was always so cheerful and vivacious. She was clearly among the living while the rest of us were not. I lifted the phone off the counter.

"Sonja! It's Mom. How are you?"

"Not good, Mom."

"The nurse who answered was so friendly. They sure have a friendly staff, don't you think?"

I smiled into the phone. I was not going to let her in on the fact that a patient answered her call; no nurse would be that friendly. And no phone calls went to the nurses' stations anyway because they were too busy. There was a phone in the hallway for our calls.

"Yep, she's amazing." Which was true, just not for the reasons my mom thought.

"I've been thinking about you all week."

"Thanks, Mom. So, how are you?" I asked.

"Good! I went on a walk with my neighbor, Bethany, went to the store, and now I'm just dropping treats off to some neighbors."

I cut her off. "Mom, someone needs to use the phone. I've got to go." I just could not hear about her list of activities that day.

Coming home from the hospital, I was still in terrible shape. I was now well-aware that, for mental illness, hospitals don't cure people in the same way they cure a broken hip or heart failure. Once you have been diagnosed, the hospital is where you go if you are a threat to yourself or others. Sometimes they tweak your medications, but a lot of times, after three to four days, they let you go with the same problems you had before you went in. As I look back now, people would often say to me, "You need to get help, Sonja," and I would remind them that I had tried dozens of medications, seen countless different therapists, was regularly hospitalized, and had a strong support network. So, what was this additional help they were referring to?

# CHAPTER 44

# Allyson's Phone Call

The tension in my marriage increased with my spending, and Mitch realized paying off my credit cards was not a permanent fix. The next credit card statement rolled in at a dangerously high number, and Mitch pushed it back to me.

"Sonja, I'm not paying this off. For the first time in your life take responsibility of your debt."

"But I have no job, no money, no way to pay it off!" I shouted and followed him out of the room.

"We've talked about this enough for you to know my answer to that. Return the jewelry," he snapped.

"You know I can't do that."

I teared up. For him it was an obvious fix: return the jewelry and pay off the credit cards. But my obsession with each item ran so deep that I knew once I returned an item, I would be sent on another wild goose chase to find it and purchase it all over again.

"I've enabled you. I shouldn't have paid off your spending for so many years. I can't have you bankrupt the family because you want to buy jewelry," he said quietly. Mitch was exhausted with my spending, and so was I. All at once I felt the weight of my spending. It felt as if every dollar of my $150,000 in charges had fallen on me in pennies.

For months, I let the bills arrive. I shoved the envelopes in my dresser drawer, unopened. Even though the interest was compounding at a steady rate, I continued to avoid every aspect of my spending. The credit card companies called nonstop, but I never answered their calls. So, the banks sent persistent debt collectors after me. I told myself I wasn't going to answer until I had a plan.

I privately filed for bankruptcy, but once Mitch found out, he told me I did not qualify and had it dismissed. I was sunk. I didn't know how I was going to solve my debt problem. It only added to the already massive burden I walked around with in this life and created even more anxiety. The debt collectors started calling me daily. One day I almost didn't answer the phone until I realized it was Allyson.

"Sonja, I have to tell you something." Her voice was stern.

"What?" I asked, scared of what was coming next.

"I have stage-four melanoma cancer in my lung and brain."

I held my mouth with my hand. "Is there a treatment for it?"

"The doctor said there's no cure. There's a trial drug, Keytruda, I can try, but there's no guarantee it'll help. I'm dying."

Everything in my whole being fought that word, "dying." I refused to accept it. An anger so fierce burned that my throat felt on fire.

"Mom's flying out and we're driving to Minnesota so I can get my treatments at Mayo Clinic."

"I'll meet you guys there. I love you, Allyson." The words seemed hollow; they didn't even begin to describe my feelings toward my sister.

In my heartbreak, I explicitly felt distrust in God's "bigger plan" and loving hand. How could anything this bitter be out of love, and how would her death be for anyone's greater good?

Allyson had five children and her youngest was three. Would he even remember her?

My heart screamed at God: "How could You? How could You take her from me?" I pounded the carpet harder and harder, like a child purging a tantrum. I had believed my whole life that God gave me Allyson as a tender mercy, and now He was taking my gift away. I was angry at God.

Even though she had children who depended on her more than I did, I felt just as needy as her three-year-old. She was the one person who could reach into my illness and pull out Sonja, making me see reason when I was my sickest and most delusional. Allyson had access to my sanity. Why would God want to take her away when He knew I couldn't survive without her?

A few days later, I tossed my duffel bag into the airplane over-head storage. The setting sun glared through the window. I violently yanked the visor down, immediately silencing the light. All my anger melted into deep sadness, and I did my best to stop crying before arriving at the Mayo Clinic.

The place was gorgeous, with tall glass ceilings and well-dressed patients. It was easy to forget we were in a hospital. I ran to Allyson and my mom. We all hugged each other before we entered the doc-tor's office, where a man in a nice suit waited for us. All the doctors wore suits instead of lab coats at the Mayo Clinic.

"I'm Dr. Harris." He shook our hands and turned to Allyson. "Your diagnosis is terminal."

We all sat in shock hearing the words out loud. My mom broke down crying. Dr. Harris continued, "Keytruda is a newly approved drug but not for your diagnosis. We'll try it anyway to give you more time. I won't lie to you, this is going to be a nasty fight, but you can decide when you're done."

I could not believe what I was hearing, and to be honest, I was jealous. No one had ever told me I got to decide when I had had enough of my illness, and I couldn't imagine what it would be like to have an out like that—a doctor's note that allowed me to say when I was done fighting for my life.

Yet, Allyson did fight. She had the gamma knife take out the two tumors in her brain; she had radiation on the tumor as big as a tennis ball in her lung. She had nine tumors cut out of her small intestines. Then the experimental drug Keytruda filled her veins every three weeks. The question of how long we had left with Allyson weighed heavily on me.

I went home and Lincoln told me he'd gotten a B on his biology test. Lincoln was a consistent straight-A student, so I was more than a little surprised.

The next day Lincoln and I met with his biology teacher after school.

"Lincoln did very well. He didn't miss any questions on the multiple choice section." She pulled out his test and pointed to the essay portion. "His essay responses were just a little too short." They didn't seem sparse to me, but I was willing to go with it.

"Okay." I nodded. "Lincoln, why don't you meet with your teacher before the next test and go over the study guide and essays."

"I can do that," Lincoln agreed.

On the next test, he got another B. The rage that had been simmering in me since Allyson's diagnosis unleashed my current manic episode into epic proportions. Before school started that next morning I drove to Lincoln's school and walked straight into his teacher's classroom.

"Show me the test," I demanded. His teacher looked shocked that I came to her room unannounced. "Show me what he got wrong."

She got Lincoln's test out and flipped to the back. "He didn't have enough on his essay questions."

I looked down at the lengthy paragraphs he had written. "Okay, so what information is missing?"

"I don't know, he just needs more," she said.

"What more could he have written?" I challenged.

"Just more."

"More what? Are you grading this on length or content?" I sounded annoyed.

The teacher had no answer.

"You're just taking points off! Give him the points back!" I yelled. Her eyes got big. "I'm not joking. Give him all three points back on each essay question."

"I've never done that before."

"Well, you're going to do it now." I folded my arms.

She got silent.

"This is how it's going to happen. I'll file a complaint against you to the principal. Then I'll rally all the other parents, and we'll put a story about you in the newspaper." I leaned over her desk. "Trust me. It's in your best interest to just give him the points back."

She got out a pen and gave Lincoln full credit on the essay questions. The bell rang for school to start, and students lined up at her door.

A male teacher came in. "Are you okay?" he asked Lincoln's teacher. I'm sure he heard my yelling. She didn't say anything. "You need to leave. School's started," the male teacher told me.

"That's fine. I got what I needed," I said, pushing past him on my way out.

Although I had never behaved this intensely with one of my kids' teachers before, I felt justified. Being in a manic episode felt so good that no one else's perspective or feelings seem to matter. Mania creates an intoxicating feeling that you are one hundred percent right in the way you see everything and that you have the power to make anything happen. It felt like a real-life Liquid Luck, from the Harry Potter series. I could buy a lottery ticket every day, and every day I would fully expect that it was a winner. Your confidence is so believable that others easily buy into your story, and if they don't, you charm or intimidate them to remove them as an obstacle, but not without consequences.

A week later a letter from the school district came banning me from school property. Not being permitted on school property was something that had happened to my dad. One would think that going through the experience, I would logically say, *Wait, this is a manic episode just like dad went through. I should reconsider my feelings and make a better choice,* or some internal narrative like that. But when you are in a manic state, there is no reflection or learning from the past because everything inside you is shouting that your feelings are one hundred percent real.

Mania was the ugly bullying side of the illness that I was not willing to address, mostly because it was an amazing and addictive high. So, I took the letter, shoved it in my dresser drawer along with my credit card bills, and proceeded with my pain-ridden day without another thought about the incident.

I continued to push Lincoln's schedule with clocklike precision, as if he was a cog in a Swiss watch. I needed him to keep up with my pace, so he could meet all his goals. But I wasn't working with cogs and springs. I was working with a person, and one day I pushed Lincoln beyond any human's natural limits.

"Mom, please cancel the tennis match today!" Lincoln pleaded.

"No, I'm not doing that!"

"Move it back just one hour. I need one short break today. Just one."

"An hour is not a short break, Lincoln. You need to learn how to sacrifice for your goals. That's what truly successful people do."

He stood up and in a measured, firm voice said, "No, I'm done." Months of pushing finally came to a head.

"Lincoln, you're only hurting yourself. My life stays the same whether you become better at tennis or not. Your choices affect your life!"

Lincoln cried, and I knew he felt conflicted with wanting to meet his goals, but I hadn't realized I pushed him far beyond his capabilities.

He ran out the door into the cold night. He ran and ran until I couldn't catch up to him. It was early December, and the roads were icy, but he continued to run until he disappeared in the falling snow. I frantically called Mitch, who came home from work. We called friends and neighbors, and he was not there. I freaked out, and Mitch explained to me the metaphor that "a bow that is constantly strung will lose its spring." He was asking that I give Lincoln the space to be a kid.

Mitch drove around the neighborhood and nearby parks but to no avail. Two hours later we heard the front door open. Lincoln came home. He had been outside that whole time. We immediately hugged him. "We love you, Lincoln." I said.

Mitch walked Lincoln into the living room and turned on the gas fireplace. Lincoln lay down in front of it. Mitch took a blanket and laid it over him. He then lay down on the floor right next to Lincoln with his arm around him, and said, "I'm sorry, Lincoln. Help me understand what you're feeling." Lincoln nodded, and they both stayed on the floor in silence until he was ready to talk. I sat quietly on the couch. This was my fault and shame filled me, yet I didn't know how to change.

# CHAPTER 45

# Flowers

How have you been since we last met?" my therapist, Dr. Randall, asked.

"I want to resign and give my family my two-week notice. I need to die." I said.

"Sonja, suicide is very selfish."

"Do you even see my pain? No, I don't think you do. I think it's selfish of you and my family to insist I stay when I'm in this much pain. Plus, they'd be better off without me."

"That's distorted thinking. They need you. Things will get better."

"When? No one can tell me *when*! I hate my life."

"Think of one thing you like about life besides your family."

"*The Ellen DeGeneres Show*. She makes me laugh."

"That's great. You should plan times throughout the week specifically dedicated to the Ellen show. What else?"

"I like flowers."

"Then your homework this week is to buy some flowers and enjoy them. Can you do that?"

I shrugged. "Probably not."

"Can you at least try?"

"I'm really good at trying things. Just know that if you want success with me, you're not going to get it. Failure, that's more my style."

"I'll take your trying. Go buy flowers and try to enjoy them."

Flowers. That was what my therapist thought could save me—thin petals and long stems. I wanted to believe that would work, but I was doubtful. Still, I was going to try his suggestion and give it all I had.

I leaned my head against the car window as Mitch drove Lincoln and me to Home Depot to buy flowers. My eyes scanned the scenery passing by, although I was not taking a single thing in.

"When is Chase coming over?" Lincoln asked.

"We need to pick him up after we go to Home Depot," I responded with my forehead still pressed against the window.

"We're tight on time. Can't his dad bring him?" Mitch asked, a bit irritated. I ignored him, lost in my thoughts.

"Jump out of the car!" my brain screamed at me. "Open the door and throw yourself out." I pressed my head harder against the car window as if I was trying to smash the thoughts away.

"Hello? Sonja?" Mitch's voice broke through my thoughts.

"Just roll with it," was all I could mutter back. I didn't have the energy to explain that I told Chase's mom I would pick him up because she was working, and her husband would have to pack all their little kids into the car just to bring Chase over. We didn't have small children to deal with, so it would be easier for us to do it.

We walked into the Home Depot nursery. Mitch pushed the cart behind me as I placed cartons of roses, marigolds, and mums in the basket. I hoped my therapist was right about this. I bought enough flowers to fill our entire front yard. I spent days outside in my big hat with my hands in the dirt planting a bounty of flowers. I became a landscaping expert overnight, and all my neighbors wanted to know whom I hired to landscape my yard.

Journal Entry
*December 11, 2015*

I reached out to touch my roses hoping to feel the beauty of my favorite flower. I felt nothing. My fingers snapped the stem in half. Why did I go outside? Did I really think I could break through the glass wall my mind builds around me? I dropped the rose on the ground and turned my back on the beautiful day.

My mind is going crazy. People ask me what that means, but if you have to ask, you don't know what it feels like. I feel so uncomfortable inside, it's like wearing clothes that are too tight, but you can't take them off.

Truth is, I don't know how many more days I have left in me. It scares me. I want to plead with doctors, researchers, medicine companies, and investors to help save us—the mentally ill. "Please keep working hard to help us. I'm counting on you to save my life. Please hurry!" I would beg. Yet I wonder, do they see us? Do they hear our cries? Our screams? Time is running out for me.

# CHAPTER 46

# Broken Vows

*December 15, 2015*

I t was one of those nights when Lincoln and I were fighting about his schedule, and it instantly escalated to a battle of wills.

"Lincoln, I've had enough! Just do your homework!"

"I can do it later. I want to go with my friends."

"Follow the schedule, Lincoln!"

"I'm sixteen years old. I can plan my own schedule."

"No, you can't!" I couldn't fathom giving up the only thing I could control even though I knew he was fully capable of doing it and certainly old enough.

Mitch tried to mediate. "Guys, knock it off! There's no need to keep screaming at each other. This is not a hard problem to solve. Sonja, let Lincoln write out his own schedule."

"Absolutely not!"

"Sonja! Seriously, you have got to stop this! This is insane," Mitch said. He was fading. Even the years before these latest episodes I had been so sick that whether it was financially, emotionally, or spiritually, I was taking everything Mitch had and then some.

"I think I should write my own schedule!" Lincoln yelled back.

"NO!" I screamed.

"Sonja, you're done overseeing it! He's writing his own schedule!" Mitch ended the fight.

All my control was gone. In that moment, the invisible burdens caused an enormous amount of emotion to pulse through my veins, and I knew it would not be long before it unleashed. I felt like I was trapped in a building that was quickly catching fire; the flames climbed and I could feel the heat at my ankles. My pain screamed its way through the windows, like pressurized heat blowing up the glass. I knew the only way out would be to jump, so I ran to my bathroom, locked the door, unscrewed the lids to my medication, and swallowed hundreds of pills.

"Sonja, open the door," Mitch demanded.

He shook the doorknob. I ignored him.

"Sonja!" Mitch screamed. I could hear him trying to pick the lock, so I took more pills faster. I began to feel strange; my knees went weak, and I fell to the floor, straining to focus my eyes. I was sinking, slipping. My phone lit up with a text from Lorie.

*Are we still going to dinner?*

My shaky hands grabbed my phone and texted Lorie.

*Can't go. I just took a ton of pills.*

I tried calling my brother Mike and my two sisters to tell them goodbye. Heidi picked up first, and through sobs and slurred speech, I told her how much I loved her, then hung up.

I was dying. I felt it. My spirit screamed out, "Wait! Wait! I can't go. I'll never see my children again! Mitch, what would he do without me?" My family would be shattered if things ended this way. I started fighting like hell to stay alive, but I made a choice from which there was no coming back.

"Sonja!" Mitch pushed the door open.

Though my eyes kept closing, I saw him run toward me. He held my head as he called 911. Lorie and her husband, Dean, ran through the door. I went in and out of consciousness as Lorie stuck her finger down my throat trying to make me vomit. Dean called his son to come pick up Lincoln. Mitch didn't want Lincoln to see what was happening and wanted him away from the house before the ambulance arrived.

"Sonja, stay awake. We need to get these pills out." Lorie put her finger down my throat again. "Try to stay awake." I passed out quickly, and she stopped, afraid I would end up choking.

An ambulance came, and Mitch rode with me to his hospital, the University of Missouri. Dean and Lorie followed in their own car. The hospital staff immediately recognized us as the ambulance team pushed my unconscious body through the emergency room door with Mitch at my side.

I was taken to the trauma bay in the hospital, reserved for the most serious emergency room admissions. Mitch, Lorie, and Dean sat in the room with me while doctors and nurses tried to save my life. They cut all my clothes off and began pumping my stomach. The doctors filled my stomach with charcoal, hoping it could absorb some of the pills. I was immediately put on a ventilator to make sure I would not stop breathing. No one knew if I would live.

Mitch, Dean, and an ER doctor, who was a member of our church, pulled the curtain closed and gave me a blessing as I lay there unconscious. Mitch prayed, "I bless you that your relationship with Lincoln will be restored. And I bless you, Sonja"—his voice trembled—"that you will live."

I woke up three days later totally confused. I couldn't speak. What was wrong with my voice? I squinted. Everything was blurry. I couldn't move. Was I paralyzed? Where was I?

A nurse came to my side when she saw me wake up. "Sonja, you are in the ICU."

"Cazrex." I tried to speak, but nothing came out except scattered words. The nurse went and got a piece of paper and a pencil. Barely holding the pencil, my hand slid across the paper, making a crooked line. I had no control over my limbs. Had I been in a car wreck? I wanted to ask them if I would ever walk or talk again, but I blacked out.

"Sonja . . . Sonja." A nurse kept saying my name as she shook me. I opened my eyes, not realizing I had slipped back into unconsciousness and another day had passed. I saw Mitch standing next to a team of doctors.

"Mitch, you're here." I struggled to speak louder than a whisper. "How bad was the car accident?" Everyone in my room stopped and looked at me. "Am I paralyzed?"

"You're not paralyzed," was the question Mitch chose to answer.

One of the doctors stepped toward my bed. "Sonja, you tried to kill yourself. We think you took over two hundred pills. You're lucky to be alive."

It all came flooding back to me the moment he said it. Oh, my *hell*! I tried to kill myself! I wanted to scream. That was the *one thing* I had made a pact with God about, and He broke it. Panicked, I looked at Mitch for assurance, but when I looked into his eyes, it was the first time he had nothing to give.

Another doctor then spoke. "You're in no condition to be a mother right now." What did he mean? What was he talking about? Being a mother is the only thing that had given me purpose.

"Sonja, Lincoln is moving to Utah and is going to finish high school there. I gave him the option of moving to Utah to live with Chris and Leslie or to live with me in an apartment here in Columbia. He wants to go to Utah. I think being around his cousins and grand-parents might be better for him right now," Mitch told me.

I felt my whole soul being ripped into shreds, and a hundred thoughts flooded my mind. My sixteen-year-old son was being taken away from me. Would he forgive me? What would this do to his life long term? If I could not be a mother, what was I?

"We will be back to check on you tomorrow," a doctor said and headed for the door as the others followed him out.

Mitch sat in a chair by my bed; he had a hard time looking at me. But from his profile, I noticed the scruff on his face. He had not shaved for a few days.

"I love you," I said, breaking the silence.

He sighed and tightly pinched the bridge of his nose. "I love you too, Sonja. I just can't do what we've been doing anymore." He looked at the tubes in my arms. "All this . . . chaos. I sat in this room with our son while you were unconscious. Lincoln asked me if his mother would live, and I had to tell him the truth—I didn't know."

"Mitch, I'm so sorry." I choked up.

"For years you have leaned on me to fill you up, but nothing is filling *me* up. I'm so low that I'm even disinterested in living life. I've just been trying to survive and keep our family from coming apart. But now that's happened." Mitch shifted in his seat and took a breath. "I'm going to look for an apartment. You can live in the house. It'll be better for you to be around familiar things and not have to move."

"We're separating?" My heart fell to the floor, hitting the ground hard, sinking lower than ever before. I no longer believed in rock bottom.

"Sonja, I love you, how can I not? You're the mother of my children. Even with your illness, you've always put the kids first, and I've admired that about you. But I think it'd be best for both our long-term health if you learned to live a more independent life."

"What do you mean by independent?" I softly asked.

"Maybe you need to get a job. Something that requires you to wake yourself up in the morning or to shower more often. I just can't keep being the only person keeping things sane."

I knew Mitch's loss of Lincoln broke something in him. He loved me, and I loved him, but keeping the family together was a huge motivator for him to push through the many sick days and bad years.

"Are you going to divorce me?" I asked.

"I'm not sure how this will play out. I haven't thought that far ahead."

"I'd understand if you do." I swallowed. "And I'll let you go peacefully." It hurt to admit that divorcing me made sense. Unlike the two hundred pills I had taken, admitting I was a burden was much harder to swallow. All my windows had been blown out and remained opened. I looked hard at Mitch and saw him more clearly than I had ever seen him before.

"I believe God is proud of you. You've stuck with me through thick and thin, and I'm grateful for that. I don't want to cause you any more pain. But, I will fight for you, our marriage, and our family. I love you. You're my soul mate. I will do whatever I have to do to keep you." I reached my hand as far out as I could to his, but he did not move to bridge the gap. He seemed to struggle to be hopeful that things could be fixed. His phone started ringing.

"Yeah, Linc? All right. I'll be home soon." He put his phone in his pocket and looked at me briefly. "I have to go."

He got up, and every reason I had to stay alive walked out the door. I was losing everything that meant anything to me in one day. I was alone. No God. No angels. No family. I had committed the one act I swore I wouldn't, and the consequences were more than I could bear.

# CHAPTER 47

# Calm After the Storm

For the first time in twenty-two years, I was not suicidal. I had no suicidal thoughts, feelings, or emotions, and it felt foreign. I lay in the hospital bed, waiting for them to come, but they never did. I closed my eyes and just enjoyed each moment that passed. It felt wonderful. The hospital psychiatrist walked into my room.

"How are we doing today?"

"Still no suicidal feelings or thoughts. My life has fallen apart, but I want to live. I don't understand it," I said.

"The doctors think you had a seizure in the ER and that could have reset your brain like electric shock treatment does. But, to be honest, we are not one hundred percent sure what happened," she said.

"I don't need to know how or why. I'm just so grateful I feel good."

"You are so lucky to be alive and without any permanent disabilities."

"That's what everyone keeps telling me."

"You have a lot of work ahead, and you must believe you can do it. Are you willing to deal with your father's suicide?"

A flood of emotions freely flowed through me, and I allowed them to be there as tears started streaming down my cheeks. "Yes. I'm ready to let him go and forgive him for how he left."

"Good. Now, I know your sister is dying from cancer, and you've been grieving her. But why grieve a person who is still living? Be grateful she is still with you and enjoy her while you can. Celebrate every day she is alive and leave the grieving for when she actually is gone."

"I never thought about it that way, but you're right. She is here today, alive. I like that thought."

"What about your suicide attempt? How are you dealing with that?"

"Didn't see it coming. I sincerely believed I would never try to take my own life," I said.

"Yet, dying is all you thought and talked about. Can you honestly say you're surprised?"

"Yes."

"Why? You've told everyone you wanted to be dead. Was that a lie?"

I stayed quiet.

"Your illness wanted you dead, but I'm asking if you, *Sonja*, wanted to die?"

"I stayed alive for my family." I sidestepped the question.

"True, but there's more. Sonja, you've been battling suicidal thoughts and urges for over two decades. That's one amazing battle you've been in. Why have you stayed alive, dig deeper."

I choked up. The truth could no longer be hidden. "I've wanted to live," I admitted.

The psychiatrist handed me a box of Kleenex. "We are not sending you to the psych ward since you are no longer a danger to yourself. But, you need to get into an intensive outpatient program."

"I can do that."

As my psychiatrist left, my nurse walked in to check my vitals. I held back tears.

"My husband might be divorcing me," I told him.

"I divorced my first wife four years ago."

"Are you happy in your second marriage?"

"I am." He smiled.

"What if your first wife would've fought for you? Would you still have divorced her?" I asked.

"Absolutely not. I would still be married to her, but she was not fighting for me or our marriage, and that was the problem."

"I'm going to fight for my husband and our marriage. Do you think he'll stay with me?"

"I can't really say." He took the blood pressure cuff off my arm. "But I will tell you this, you're lucky to be alive. I'm a believing Christian, and people who kill themselves go to hell. You just escaped damnation." He patted my shoulder.

I knew I hadn't just escaped damnation, what I had escaped was death. The stigma around suicide and mental illness wasn't only perpetuated by those who knew little about it. Doctors working in that field were equally susceptible to bias, despite their exposure and knowledge.

While I was in the hospital, a leading psychiatrist at the University of Missouri told my husband to never bring me back to this hospital again. He told Mitch that because he was CEO he needed to take me to a hospital far away from Columbia where people didn't know us. This disturbed me on so many levels. I wondered where this psychiatrist's compassion was for my husband as a human being? He had just almost lost his wife to suicide.

And why wouldn't this psychiatrist want to use this opportunity to show that mental illness is no respecter of persons? The fact is it doesn't matter what race, religion, gender, age, or economic background you come from —royalty to the homeless—mental illness can affect anyone's family. This psychiatrist's words lit a fire inside of me. I no longer wanted to hide, but bravely stand with the mentally ill. I pondered these new feelings as I waited for Lorie to come take me home.

"You ready to go, girlfriend?" Lorie smiled as she walked into my room. She had visited me every day and was my anchor.

As we drove home, I felt nervous to see Lincoln. He never came and visited me except the one time when I was unconscious. I was also anxious to be home with Mitch again. I wanted to prove myself to him. I just wasn't sure if he would give me the chance.

I sat in my empty house when my doorbell rang. I opened the door and there stood a neighbor I had only talked to a few times in passing. I was sure that she and the entire neighborhood knew of my attempted suicide. A team of paramedics loading my unconscious body into a blaring ambulance parked in my driveway was probably hard to miss. I stood there without saying anything, and looked at her.

"I know you're not okay. Can I come in?" she tenderly asked.

"Sure." I moved to the side, and we sat on my dining room chairs.

"How are you holding up?"

I instantly broke down. "Not sure. I'm losing my son. He's sixteen. And my husband's considering divorce." I took in a shaky breath. "I'm not sure where to go from here."

"When I got diagnosed with breast cancer I thought my life would end. But then one night I told my friends I felt like I was climbing my own personal Mount Everest, and I didn't know if I was going to make it. They told me, 'If you're climbing Mount Everest, then we'll be your gloves, your boots, and your jacket along the journey.'" My neighbor teared up. "There will be people who will surround you and help you climb your own Mount Everest."

She gave me a tight hug before leaving. I was touched and surprised.

Hours rolled by, and I anxiously anticipated when Lincoln would come home from school. Because of me, he had to leave everything he cared about—parents, home, tennis, debate team—not to mention countless friends. It pained me to think back on how hard he had been working the last eight months to make the top three on the varsity tennis team, and now he'd have to leave it all behind. Mitch told me Lincoln was strong, but even so, he cried when he met with the tennis coach and told him he was leaving. I couldn't help but think that would make him resent and even possibly hate me. Although he could find reasons in my actions to deny it, I held on to the thought that despite it all, Lincoln knew I loved him.

I heard him drop his backpack on the kitchen floor and open the fridge. I quickly jumped out of bed and walked into the kitchen. He paused and looked at me before I threaded my arms around his neck. "Lincoln, I'm so sorry."

"It'll be okay." He stiffly patted my back.

"You really think so?" I asked, tearing up.

"Yeah." He turned away from me.

The doorbell rang, and a man with my oxygen tank waited on the porch. I now had all the equipment necessary to match what I always claimed to be my one-hundred-year-old self. The only thing I lacked now was a walker with tennis balls on the bottom and some more wrinkles.

"I'll be in my room packing," Lincoln said, checking a text message. I watched him go into his room and my heart snapped. The tears came and there was no way to hold them in. I looked at the man with my oxygen tank and pointed to the front room, unable to get any words out.

"It's a pretty simple setup." The man put the box on the rug. "You'll want to make sure to turn this knob."

I continued to sob.

"And then move . . ." His voice faded out as I burst into another sob in the middle of his explanation.

"Ma'am, are you all right?" He raised an eyebrow.

"Just keep going." I waved my hand for him to finish.

He cautiously continued, "You'll use this at night since you stop breathing when you sleep."

I covered my face with my hands and slid down to the rug.

He stopped again. "Ma'am, are you sure you're okay?"

I nodded, unable to speak through my tears. When he finished, he handed me the instruction manual and wished me a good day. I closed the door and went into Lincoln's room to help him pack. I ended up lying on the floor, unable to do anything but cry. I was paralyzed by sadness, and he silently continued to pack. How was anything ever going to be okay again? I picked my phone up from the bed and dialed Lorie's number.

"Lorie, we need to pack, but I can't," I cried into the phone. "I can't believe this is happening."

"I'm coming over."

Minutes later, Lorie walked through the front door and came straight into Lincoln's bedroom, where she saw Lincoln stretched out on the bed texting and me crying, helplessly moving hangers around but not accomplishing much.

"Okay, enough crying." Lorie clapped her hands. "Lincoln, you need a haircut, and I think we could all use some frozen yogurt." Lincoln and I just stared at her sudden but welcome direction. "Come on, you two, let's go," she said.

Lorie got Lincoln and me in her car and drove us to Supercuts. We sat in the waiting room while Lincoln got his haircut. He chatted with the hairdresser as if nothing was wrong.

"Is he going to be okay?" I asked Lorie.

"Sonja, he'll be more than okay," she said confidently.

"But I did this, Lorie. He's going to need therapy. This is bad. I mean, really bad!" I started getting myself worked up again.

"Kids are resilient. You need to be strong for him, for your family."

"It's not only Lincoln I need help repairing. It's my marriage. And Rachael and Alex don't even know yet."

"Just take it one day at a time," Lorie said.

My crying tapered down and all that remained were puffy eyes as I quietly ate my frozen yogurt. Back home, Lorie helped finish packing Lincoln's suitcases and set them by the front door.

That night when Mitch came home, I quickly got up to meet him at the door.

"Hi, Mitch! Are you hungry? Should I make some dinner for you?" I eagerly asked.

"No, that's okay. I'm just going to go to bed," Mitch said a bit distantly.

"Well, how was your day?" I asked, following him into our bedroom.

Mitch stopped me in the doorway. "I think it would be best if we slept in separate rooms."

In all the years we had been married, Mitch and I never let a fight put one of us in a separate bedroom. After all the arguments and crazy things I had done, Mitch had always allowed us to go back to the way we were once it was over. This time was different. Mitch needed space. I tucked myself into Alex's bed, hooked up my oxygen tank, and tried my best to sleep as I awaited the dreaded flight to Utah the next morning.

On the plane, Mitch and Lincoln chatted, and I looked out the window, feeling I would be the outsider this Christmas. We pulled into Mitch's parents' driveway and I looked at the Christmas lights on the house.

His parents were tied at the hip, as seen in the details of their home. Their shared hobby of oil painting covered the walls. Farm scenes signed by him and flower paintings signed by her. Two comfy chairs sat closely together in the front room by the fireplace where they spent their evenings, and stacks of books in the kitchen showed their shared love of French cooking. Mitch's dad, Lyle, was a lifelong student who at age sixty learned how to play the piano and at eighty started learning the violin.

"Welcome. Mr. Lincoln, you look like a man," Lyle's voice rumbled. He opened his arms to Lincoln. "Come here, my boy."

Mitch's parents were easy to be around and even easier to love. His dad was a farmer with hard hands and a soft heart, and his mom was an angel with a halo of thick white hair and perfectly manicured nails.

"Hey, Dad." Mitch hugged his dad.

"Sonja, it's good to see you." Mitch's mom, Lynne, warmly turned to me.

"Thanks for having us." I hugged her.

"Sonja, come here, dear." Lyle pulled me aside into the living room. "I want to tell you that I can't even begin to imagine what you've been through, but we're here for you and Mitch." He put his sturdy hand on my shoulder. "I just wanted you to know that."

"Thank you." I looked into the familiar blue eyes that Mitch had inherited from him.

"We love you." His voice cracked, and he quickly patted my back and walked out, cutting off any chance for me to witness the tough cowboy tear up.

I carried my bag down the stairs and saw that Mitch and Lincoln had set their bags in the same room. It did not come as a shock to me that Mitch still planned on separate rooms, but setting my bag in an empty room all alone furthered the distance Mitch continually placed between us. I wanted us to go back to normal, which I knew was a lot to ask, but that did not change my yearning for it.

"So, Mom and I are going to do some Christmas shopping tonight. Is there anything we should remember?" Mitch cheerfully asked Lincoln. With everything that had gone on, we never got around to making Christmas lists.

"I don't know." Lincoln shrugged. "Anything's good."

Like the functional, happy parents we were not, we left the house and drove to the mall.

"What do you think we should get him?" I asked Mitch.

"There are a few places I want to stop in the mall. I think they'll have something he'll like." Mitch readjusted his hands on the steering wheel. That was the most he had talked to me since I had come home from the hospital. His lengthy sentence excited me, giving me hope for longer conversations. Maybe Christmas shopping for Lincoln would give him a reason to shorten the distance he held me at.

We walked into the mall, and every banister was laced with fake pine. A larger-than-life tree shimmered in the center of the mall with ornaments the size of my head. Even though all the candy canes and trees were fake, every detail was an effort to make Christmas become something tangible.

"Wow, look at the tree." I pointed.

"Yeah. It's neat." Mitch was polite but measured in his response. He quickly turned the corner, and I sped up to follow him.

"Should we stop at Build-A-Bear? I know he's sixteen, but he still loves those things."

Mitch could sense my eagerness to get along and patch things up, and it made him uncomfortable. "I just . . . I need space away from you," he said sharply. I instantly got quiet. "I'm not trying to be mean. I just need time."

And just like that, I was reminded of his fragility and of how I had broken him. Maybe it was the cheerful people shopping around me, or how he had talked to me in the car, or maybe it was the intoxicating smell of Cinnabon around the corner, but I really believed Mitch was going to come around.

"Okay." I swallowed. "Just call me when you're ready to leave." I turned around and sat on a bench under some plastic mistletoe. And just like that, I was reminded of my own fragility.

On Christmas morning, Mitch's parents made a beautiful breakfast. Buttery waffles, bacon, and fresh orange juice waited for us on the round table.

"Good morning, Christmas crew!" Lynne greeted us as we came up the stairs.

"Merry Christmas," Mitch said before he grabbed a waffle. During breakfast Lincoln's eyes continually shifted to the shiny boxes under the tree.

"Once we're done eating, we'll open presents," I told him.

He picked up his fork and started eating at lightning speed. "I'm done."

Mitch chugged a glass of orange juice and moved to the tree. "So, these ones are yours, Lincster." Lincoln opened his Star Wars BB-8 robot and Build-A-Bear from Mitch and unwrapped the stack of clothes from me.

"Thanks, guys!" he said, looking through his gifts.

"This one is addressed to you, Mitchell." Lyle handed Mitch a small, wrapped rectangle. "From Sonja," he said.

I sat up, feeling a bit nervous as Mitch tore off the paper and pulled out a book.

He read the cover aloud. "Mitch Wasden's Missionary Journal."

"I finally had your journals from your church mission in Scotland typed out a few months ago and printed it in a hardcover book. I already sent Rachael and Alex each a copy to read while they're on their missions," I said.

"Thanks, Sonja." He smiled as he thumbed through the pages.

I sat awkwardly in my chair as Lyle looked under the tree for my gift from Mitch. It didn't take long for him to realize there weren't any other gifts.

"Well, Merry Christmas, folks," Lyle said.

For the first time in a long time I was fighting *for* Mitch instead of fighting with him, but my efforts didn't seem to be making much of a difference. I knew his emotions were complex. I had almost left him by attempting suicide, and now he was wary of getting close again.

Lincoln set up his BB-8 robot with Mitch while his parents took naps in their chairs, so I snatched the keys and drove to the cemetery to visit my dad's grave.

Snow capped the tops of every gravestone, and poinsettias spotted the white grounds with flashes of red. I stopped the car next to my father's grave and took a deep breath before I threw the car in park. I looked out my window and saw a Christmas wreath on his grave dusted in snow. Two big hearts were engraved on the dark gray stone, representing his love of my mother, his Double Double Sweetheart. From the car, I could read his motto inscribed at the bottom: FAMILY FIRST, NOTHING SECOND. He loved us so much, and although he left the way he did, his love for his family was something I could never deny.

I stepped out of the car, walked through the fresh snow, and crouched down, making myself eye level to his name on the dark gray stone. "Dad, it's taken me almost five years to get to a point where I could come and see you." Emotion swelled in my heart; tears flowed easily, and I did not hold them back. "I forgive you for how you left us. Forgive me if I didn't do enough. We both got stuck with this illness, and I don't know how, but I'm going to do something good with it, for both of us." I leaned down and kissed his ice-cold grave.

# CHAPTER 48

# Losing Lincoln

Y ou got everything?" I asked Lincoln.

"Yeah," he answered, sitting on the bed. We heard Chris and Leslie talking with Mitch's parents upstairs. They had come to pick up Lincoln. My heart stopped, and we all froze, realizing this was it. Mitch and I grabbed some of Lincoln's luggage and followed him up to the main floor.

"Lincoln, you ready to go?" Leslie cheerfully said, hugging him.

I wanted to reach out and grab Lincoln back. I wanted to scream, "No! You can't have him! He's not yours to raise!" Mitch's brother and his wife were doing us nothing but favors, yet it stung like an insult and the moment burned with heartbreak.

As I looked at Mitch and saw him cry, I realized I was not in this boat alone; we were unified in our suffering. Mitch grabbed Lincoln and hugged him tightly. Lincoln started crying. I embraced Lincoln to say goodbye. "I love you, Lincoln."

He started to cry. "I know, Mom. Just get well. I'll be fine." Lincoln's strength and fortitude were far beyond his sixteen-year-old self.

We stood and watched him get into the car with Leslie to start an entirely new life. Chris stopped at the door, and Mitch pulled his big brother close.

"Thank you, brother." Mitch cried in his arms.

Chris held Mitch tight, and I knew their already close friendship had sunk deeper. Chris was doing something for Mitch that he could not do himself, parent his child. Leslie brought us a lot of comfort because we knew Lincoln was going to be taken care of by someone fiercely loyal who would love him like her own.

Mitch and I zipped up our bags and left for the airport. We didn't talk much the whole way home—something about suffering makes silence loud. We both knew there was too much sadness wrapped around this event to talk about it without crying, and we had both cried enough.

When we got home to an empty house, Lincoln's absence stung deeper. Mitch went into our bedroom, and I went into Alex's room. There was nothing left to say. Lincoln was gone. We both lost our son. We continued to sleep in separate bedrooms while Mitch looked for an apartment, and I was starting to feel the distance between us widen.

On the verge of losing not only my son but also my husband, I drove straight to the nearest Wal-Mart and thumbed through the greeting cards. I found one of those cards that are two feet long and one foot wide with its very own giant envelope. It had a sleepy puppy on the front with big letters that read, GET WELL SOON. Years of tender feelings and reasons I loved Mitch poured out of me and into the larger-than-life card. I continued writing: "I know that having a sick wife makes you sick too. I hope you get well soon and remember how much I love you."

I taped a picture of me inside. It was a picture my college room-mate had taken of me right before I went to surprise Mitch in the middle of his history class and ask him on a date. She captured me laughing in pure happiness, something Mitch had not seen in years.

Although long years together had brought aging and complexity to our lives, I knew that not so deep down we were the same starry-eyed kids that fell for each other's smiles and longed for each other's kiss.

I went home and gripped my card, rehearsing what I would say. I found Mitch in the kitchen.

"Mitch!" I said, gathering my courage.

"Sonja, we need to talk," he interrupted.

I panicked. Oh no, he found an apartment. "Is it about you moving out?" I forced myself to ask.

"Yes. I went to sign the lease today—"

"Wait!" I shouted. "Just wait. Please read this first, before you say anything else." I pushed the giant envelope forward. "Just read it."

Mitch opened the letter, and we stood silently as he read it. He closed the card and set it on the counter when he was done. He teared up, not saying anything for a moment as he gathered his voice. "Thank you." Choked up, he leaned over and kissed my forehead.

"Did I change your mind about leaving?" I asked.

"No." He laughed.

"What?"

"Because when I went to sign the lease today, I felt like it was the absolute wrong thing to do. I walked away from it. I'm staying here with you," he said.

I hugged him. "You know, I was prepared to bake your favorite cookies every day to win you back."

"Hmm. Cookies would still be a good idea." He held up the college picture of me. "I always loved that picture of you."

"I want you to put that picture by your nightstand and remember me that way."

He pulled me back into his arms, and I was home. Staying together was the legacy we wanted to leave for our kids. In our marriage, even when the most tempting offer was to leave, we found a way to stay.

CHAPTER 49

# Dialectical Behavior Therapy (DBT)

Lorie did a ton of research and found Dialectical Behavior Therapy, which is a scientifically based therapy with excellent results. I had never heard about it. I sat in my DBT therapist's waiting room for my first visit. There were old and young people sitting alongside me in that waiting room. I saw a young mom with her two-year-old, a teenage boy listening to music, and a man with a cane leaned back in a chair next to the fish tank. Everyone was here to meet with their psychiatrist or therapist.

Mental illness touched so many people's lives. The National Alliance on Mental Illness said that one in five people are affected by mental illness in a given year. Suicide is a leading cause of death in the US. Depression is the leading disability in the world. Yet, are we, that suffer from mental disorders, talked about and funded like the number one cause of disabilities in the world? Do we attract the same level of public awareness, campaigns, fund-raisers, T-shirts, and bake sales as other physical illnesses? People don't like talking about mental disorders. The topic is more of a conversation killer than starter.

"Sonja Wasden," my DBT therapist called into the waiting room.

I stood up and walked back to the hallway of offices to my therapist's room. Tonya was in her forties and had brown hair and big eyes. She looked caring but stern, like a strong mother figure. I was ready to ask her the question I asked all my psychiatrists and therapists.

"Do you know anyone with a mental illness that is living a normal life?"

"Yes. Tons," she said in a matter-of-fact tone.

I was sure she misunderstood my question. "I'm talking about patients who deal with daily suicidal thoughts."

"Yes, I know." Tonya opened her desk drawer looking for a pen.

"I'm talking *severe* mental illness—like people who can't get out of bed or who have crazy spending sprees. People, like me, who are living an impossible life," I added.

Tonya crossed her legs. "Absolutely. Sonja, DBT changes people's lives. And there's no such thing as an impossible life."

She was the first therapist to give me a straight answer, and a positive one to boot. I had asked every psychiatrist and therapist that question, and they always seemed unwilling to commit to a solid answer. I liked Tonya's confidence, but I still felt skeptical.

"I've done twenty years of therapy, and none of it has helped," I admitted. "I've been listened to, validated, advised, and scolded. I'd feel good for a few hours after a therapy session, but my behavior and thought patterns never really changed."

"I completely understand your frustration," Tonya responded. "I was going to quit being a therapist because I didn't see my patients getting better. I felt like what I was doing was worthless."

"So what changed?" I asked.

"I learned about Marsha M. Linehan's DBT program, and its great success. I got certified and watched it change people's lives. This is scientific evidence-based therapy, and I know it works," she promised. "You put the hard work in, and you will get the skills to create a life not only worth living, but one where you will experience joy." She looked at me a little softer. "Do you want that?"

The single word—joy—left me dizzy. Never in my wildest dreams did I think I could have a joyful life. Her confidence gave me the first real hope I had in years. Tonya had me believing DBT could finally change the course of my life.

"More than anything," I said.

She taught me the four key skills in DBT. First is mindfulness. It's the ability to radically accept things as they are and be present in the moment. The second is distress tolerance, which is the ability to tolerate negative emotions instead of trying to escape from them. The third is emotional regulation, which teaches you the ability to manage and change intense and problematic emotions. The fourth is interpersonal effectiveness, which teaches you to communicate with others in a way that is assertive, maintains self-respect, and strengthens relationships.

These were all new concepts and not a single therapist had taught me them before. For the first time, I was going to learn skills to deal with my illness instead of just talking about it. Hope filled my soul. I was determined to not only learn these skills but be a master of them.

Tonya continued, "We have weekly one-on-one sessions, a two-hour group class, and twenty-four-hour coaching. Use twenty-four-hour coaching when you're in the crisis. You'll have my phone number, and I will always respond within ten minutes."

"So, I should call when I'm suicidal?" I asked.

"Suicide is off the table. That part is nonnegotiable," she said firmly.

"How do I take it off the table?" I asked. I had always felt like that decision wasn't entirely up to me. It was my disease taking me over, and I had little say on the matter.

"Suicide is never an option," she said, rather forcefully.

"But if I get in too much pain or go into another episode, I don't know if I can survive it. I fought it with everything I had and ended up attempting."

"Look at the evidence. You've made it through every episode for over twenty years. Yes, you attempted suicide, but that's because you hadn't taken it off the table. You're sitting on this couch right now, in this room, seeking more help to create a life for yourself. You not only desperately want this—you have the determination to do it."

"But what if I don't believe I have it in me to go through another episode?" My confidence had been greatly shaken by my suicide attempt. "I don't want any more episodes or illness. I'm tired."

"This isn't about what you want," Tonya said, snapping me back into reality. "Lots of people have illnesses they don't want, but nevertheless it's theirs to deal with."

She had my full attention.

"So what are your thoughts on people who kill themselves? Like your dad?" she asked.

"I think they're at peace and out of pain," I said.

"How do you know killing yourself doesn't put you in a different type of pain?"

"Well, that's just what I believe."

"The fact is not you, I, or a single person living knows what happens to people who kill themselves. But I've often wondered, if it would be another type of hell to watch your family suffer because of something you did and not to be able to apologize or comfort them. Imagine looking down on the family you left in pieces, and you can only watch. Wouldn't that cause pain even to a heavenly being? When you hurt people you love by killing yourself, there is no closure."

"But I think being bipolar is no different than having cancer. If the illness takes you out, it takes you out," I said.

"Yes, both are biological illnesses, but every illness affects people and families differently. I've done therapy with people who have lost someone to cancer and lost someone to suicide, and there's a different type of horror with the latter. That's just a fact. You would change the course of your family's life. Do you want to be responsible for that?"

"I've never thought about it like that," I admitted.

"Well, it's time to."

# CHAPTER 50

# 24/7 DBT Coaching

On a Saturday morning, I woke up having dreamed about Mitch's and my time in Michigan during graduate school. It was a recurring nightmare, and the details were never far away: the smell of the hospital rooms, the needles, tubes of blood, apartment walls, newborn diapers, and the constant financial stress. Michigan was a painful memory for me, but it was one I couldn't seem to let go, though I knew I needed to.

"Morning, cutie," Mitch greeted.

I opened the fridge and pulled out a carton of strawberries. "Mitch, in Michigan, why didn't we go on welfare?"

He stood next to me, putting his bowl in the sink. "Sonja, lots of women work while they're pregnant."

"And most of them either have insurance or go on welfare to get it. I was seven months pregnant and hadn't seen a doctor." My voice trembled.

"Ugh, this again? Why are we reliving the past?" He sighed.

"I'm not. I just feel like you have never acknowledged how traumatic that was for me. We gambled with Rachael's life. Something could've really gone wrong!"

"But it didn't," Mitch reminded me.

"That's not the point! It was still a dumb decision."

"Are you blaming this on me?" Mitch asked.

"No! I'm blaming us!"

"I'm sorry we were poor graduate students. It wasn't an ideal situation, but we were doing our best," Mitch said calmly.

"And neither of our parents stepped in to help us!" I desperately wanted him to feel the panic I once had. "I would never let my kids be in that situation."

"Our parents did the best they could," Mitch defended.

"I want you to admit we were young and dumb. I don't want you to relive the past. I just want you to acknowledge it."

"You always regret the past. Just leave it alone."

"Maybe I keep going back because you continually brush it under the rug and act like it never happened. If you just admitted we've made mistakes—"

"I don't think that would change anything," Mitch interrupted.

"To this day when I think about it, it makes me sick. It makes me feel like we were unfit parents. We had no business having children if we couldn't afford them. We weren't being responsible."

"Well, everything worked out."

"But it doesn't always. I want us to look each other in the eyes and say we made a mistake."

"I'm more interested in the future. What are we going to do today to make better decisions?" Mitch countered.

"You don't know how to validate!" I sobbed. "I swear you need DBT therapy more than I do!"

I called Tonya in a frenzied state. "Mitch isn't validating my point of view. I want to run out of this home and never come back! He makes me escalate!" I yelled into the phone.

"Sanja, Sanja." Tonya always calmly mispronounced my name. "Do you have your stuffed animals?" I had her on speaker.

"No."

"Crying hysterically isn't going to get you anywhere."

"But Mitch won't validate my feelings!"

"Sanja! Stop. Where are your stuffed animals?" she asked.

"In my room," I answered.

"Okay. Go get them. We don't want to end up in the ER. Now, I don't want you interacting with Mitch."

"Because Mitch just escalates me!" I said, glaring at him.

"No, Sanja, this isn't about Mitch. This is about you learning to interact with the people in your life, in your environment, skillfully," Tonya corrected.

"I'm trying!"

"I want you to do the TIPS skills. Go put your face in ice water and call me in ten minutes." She hung up.

Mitch filled a bowl with ice water and set it on the counter for me. I dunked my face. *One . . . two . . . three . . . four . . . five,* I counted in my head. The shock from the icy water immediately pulled my thoughts away from my frustration. I pulled my face out of the water and breathed. Wet hair hung around my face, and I instantly felt the cold air, like a minty breath, hit my cheeks. I leaned over the bowl and cried. I needed more dunks. I wiped my hair away and went back under. *One . . . two . . . three . . . four . . . five.* I did four more dunks and then dried my face. I poured the ice water down the sink and got in my bed with my stuffed animals.

I texted Tonya: *I'm at a 3 now. TIPS worked.*

"Sonja?" Mitch knocked at the door. I didn't say anything. He walked into our bedroom and sat at the edge of the bed. "I want to validate you. You're right, we did make mistakes, and if I could go back and change things, I would." He paused. "I don't want to acknowledge it because it's hard for me to admit I did something that hurt my wife so badly and that I didn't take care of our children the way I would have liked to." He grabbed my hand. "We're a team. We've been to hell and back and created a beautiful life together. Let's focus on our future. Can we do that?"

"Yes." I squeezed his hand. "And thank you for validating me. I won't bring it up anymore." I kissed the top of his hand. "We're a good team."

# CHAPTER 51

# Starting a Life

I knew that to get my life back, I needed to start facing the wreckage of my last episode head-on. I opened my dresser drawer and gathered every credit-card statement. I read them one by one and made myself look at the numbers. Taking in how bad my spending had gotten made it hard to identify with myself. I felt like there was me, and then this person whose credit-card bills covered my bed. I had to separate myself from that person to get through all the envelopes. I got a highlighter and marked the totals on each statement. Calling the creditors to see how I could settle my debts was an eye-opening experience. I would need a lot of money to pay these off, and I knew Mitch would not be a part of this repair.

I made a list of ways to pay it off on my own.

1. Get a job.
2. Sell jewelry.

Although my list consisted of only two things, they were large tasks to take on. Aside from being a phlebotomist I hadn't worked outside the home since college. I loved the White House Black Market clothing store and mostly wore their clothes, so I filled out an application online. My resume was sparse for my age, so I decided to go to the store to talk to the manager. She didn't know me, but the assistant manager did because I shopped there so much. They ended up offering me a job as a salesperson. I wasn't sure I could hold down a job. I could imagine myself coming in late, forgetting I had to work, or arguing with coworkers and customers. But to my surprise, none of that happened. I quickly became one of the highest selling salespeople in the store. I woke up one morning ready for another day of work.

"Sonja, can you steam these display dresses?" my manager asked. The black dress swung on the hanger as I hung it up to steam. The warm puff of smoke erased the small creases, and I slipped the dress back on the mannequin.

"Is Sonja working today?" a short woman named Julie asked. Julie had money to blow and trusted my style advice the last two times she shopped here.

"Hi, Julie." I poked my head out from behind the mannequin.

"Oh, thank heavens!" she huffed. "My husband planned a family vacation, and I need something nice to wear." A pair of pants caught her eye. "How about these?" she asked.

"Go try them on. You know I'll be honest." I smiled.

Julie slid the curtain and noisily struggled her way into the pair of pants. "I'm coming out!" she yelled. She stood in front of the mirror with her hands on her hips. "Hmm, is it just me or do these make me look wide?" she asked.

"No, they look great!" a coworker cooed.

"Sonja?" Julie raised an eyebrow.

"Yeah, they make you look a little wide," I said. "But, try these."

I handed her a few skirts in a very flattering cut. After trying on one, she asked me to pick out shoes and jewelry for them. She bought everything. I only made nine dollars an hour, which was not making a big dent in my debt, but I got so much more out of it than a paycheck. I got the confidence that perhaps I could function in the world and be more independent.

To get me ready for my next big step, Lorie and I laid all my jewelry out on the dining room table. The table sparkled with a mass array of diamonds and gold that looked too beautiful to part with. This was my treasure trove, and I felt extremely attached to it. I put on a gold-and-diamond necklace. "This really is pretty," I said to the mirror.

"Which is why it'll sell fast," Lorie said, trying to keep me on track.

"I know." I took the necklace off.

We photographed every piece, and Lorie helped me put them on eBay. It was easy to sell my gold Tiffany necklace and bracelet, but the no-name-brand stuff was difficult. I sold what I could to jewelry stores and pawnshops. To help my cause, Lorie even bought two bracelets from the pile. Jewelry was not an appreciating asset. I lost money on all of it.

Mitch saw I was making considerable efforts to pay off my credit card debt so he helped me come to settlements with the creditors. The silver lining in this ordeal was that my trashed credit score stopped credit-card companies from sending me any more offers. Mitch and I also came to an agreement on how to manage our finances, and that was to separate them completely. To this day, I do not own a credit card; I operate purely on cash and a debit card. Mitch gives me a weekly allowance, and he comes with me to buy any big purchases. I have not had a spending relapse since.

I grabbed a handful of art knives and squeezed a dozen colors out on my palette. My heart beat so fast out of excitement. I was going to paint for real and not just in my head. I sat painting for hours, forgetting to eat, check the laundry, or think about my illness. I was completely involved with my painting, and when I finished one painting, I started another one. All the chaos inside of me poured onto my canvas. I wiped my forehead, undoubtedly getting paint on myself, and looked back at my work. It was colorful, loud, and chaotic—everything my clothes and house were not, but everything I was.

I started going to hot yoga because Tonya said daily exercise would help my mental health. This idea was not something new to me, but my past attempts had little success. Since DBT was big on mindfulness, and hot yoga was a great combination of getting your

She squeezed my hand and ran with Brett through the cheering line.

"And just like that, they're gone," I said to Mitch, watching their car drive away.

"I trust him with my daughter," he said, holding my hand. This was a day I had dreamed about for years and I was grateful to be alive.

Once again, only six months later, beautiful flowers and delicious food were prepared as my son Alex married his best friend, Kelsie. She was everything I was not. Kelsie was constantly happy, calm, stable, and looked like a beautiful Disney princess. She had never experienced depression, yet she was understanding and kind to me. I always joked with her that I was clearly standing in the wrong bus line in heaven and should have joined hers. I was thrilled she was joining the family.

Their special day was held in a white shabby chic building. Baby pictures of them hung on twine over a wall, and grilled cheese sandwiches were served with chocolate chip cookies, two of Kelsie's favorite foods. I watched Alex beam throughout the day and hold his bride tight. It was clear they were in love. I danced with Alex for the mother-son dance and cried my way through it. There's something about weddings that makes you feel like you are losing something even though you're gaining so much more.

"Two kids married," I whispered to Mitch.

"And one to go." Mitch rubbed Lincoln's head.

Lincoln was tearing up. "What's wrong, Lincoln?" I put my arm around him.

He hugged me fully for the first time since he left home and whispered in my ear, "You're alive. You're here."

# CHAPTER 57

# Retirement Party

*November 24, 2017*

For Thanksgiving, we rented a cabin in the mountains near Sundance in Utah since all the kids were studying at BYU in Provo. This was our first holiday with the kids' spouses.

Our car zipped around tree-lined roads as flocks of wild turkeys scattered and the sun slipped past the horizon line. There was a soft orange glow that seemed to coat everything.

"Wow, this looks nicer than the picture!" Mitch said, pulling up to the cabin. I clicked my seat belt off and looked up at the tall cabin. "I'll get the bags. You go on in," Mitch insisted.

I opened the cabin door and saw all my kids and Mitch's parents waiting for me. The room was covered in streamers and balloons with a big sign above the fireplace that read RETIREMENT PARTY.

"Happy retirement, Mom!" Lincoln came up and hugged me.

"What's all this?" I said, a bit shocked.

"You always said once you became an empty nester you wanted a retirement party, just like anyone with a full-time career would get. So, now that Lincoln's in college, we thought it was time to celebrate!" Rachael said.

"We all wrote you a personal letter, but you can read them later." Alex handed me a stack of letters.

"Wow." I teared up.

I went to sit on the couch with Alex and Kelsie, but Lincoln stopped me. "You sit here." He pointed to a chair at the front of the room with a little tiara balanced on a small pillow.

"Oh." I got up and placed the tiara on my head. I had always loved the crowns in Barbie movies. The kids organized a few games that we played, like what was Mom's most recent Internet search or what's Mom's favorite magazine, to which the kids accurately replied *People*.

As we laughed and talked, I realized my family was happy. And so was I. Mitch often referred to our family as a tribe, and that was exactly what we were. A group of people so tight and loyal, we were like an army who had been in a foxhole together and came out alive. Nothing could sever us.

Mitch handed me a long red box, and my heart pounded. Jewelry had been the source of so much contention in our home that I doubted Mitch would ever give me another piece of jewelry again. "Sonja, I'd like to read you my letter, but first open your retirement gift."

As I opened the long rectangle box, diamonds sparkled back at me. I immediately recognized the bracelet. It was an Art Deco diamond bracelet being sold as part of an estate sale. It was the most beautiful piece of jewelry I had ever laid my eyes on. Mitch stood behind me with his right hand on my shoulder and the letter in his left.

Dear Sonja,

Happy retirement from 25 years of dedicated service as CEO of Wasden Enterprises. You have often said that you feel like you're 100 inside. You're close, but not quite there. If you add up each of the kids' ages—23, 21, and 18—plus the years you've been married at 25, you get 87 years, not quite 100. To commemorate all those years of service, we wanted to give you something that is as old as you feel but has found a way to, just like you, be timeless, stunning and beautiful. It was made during the 1930s Art Deco period, exactly 87 years from 2017. This bracelet is like you in one other important way. Each diamond was formed through a process of years of heat, pressure and refinement.

You will always be a mother. You are only retiring from the children's laundry, tennis practices, art lessons, and tutoring. Now it's your time to embark on a few dreams that you selflessly put on hold while you focused on the most important thing, raising great children. I love you and would pick you again, you were chosen for me.

Love always,
Mitter

There wasn't a dry eye in the whole room. I was emotional but more than that, I was grateful. Was I still ill? Yes. Was I still a powerless victim of my illness? No, I wasn't, not anymore.

I could have freed myself at any time and at any moment. I just never realized I held the keys to my shackles. Everything I needed I had within me. I did not need to move or get a new husband or make more money or lose weight. The people around me didn't need to change. I needed to change the way I interacted with myself.

I no longer believe I'm living an impossible life. Now instead of asking therapists if they know of anyone who has overcome suicidal thoughts or asking doctors if the mentally ill can live a life worth living, I could ask myself. And the answer was yes. I did know someone.

Me.

# End of Part One

CPSIA information can be obtained
at www.ICGtesting.com
Printed in the USA
LVHW080453291220
675296LV00015B/1536

9 781733 619493